CHANGING POLITICS IN JAPAN

CHANGING POLITICS IN JAPAN

IKUO KABASHIMA AND GILL STEEL

CORNELL UNIVERSITY PRESS
ITHACA AND LONDON

First published 2010 by Cornell University Press
First printing, Cornell Paperbacks, 2010
Printed in the United States of America

Library of Congress Cataloging-in-Publication Data

Kabashima, Ikuo, 1947–
 Changing politics in Japan / Ikuo Kabashima and Gill Steel.
  p. cm.
 Includes bibliographical references and index.
 ISBN 978-0-8014-4876-8 (cloth : alk. paper) —
 ISBN 978-0-8014-7600-6 (pbk. : alk. paper)
 1. Japan—Politics and government—1989– 2. Political parties—
Japan. 3. Political culture—Japan. I. Steel, Gill, 1965– II. Title.
 JQ1631.K23 2010
 320.952—dc22   2009049506

Cornell University Press strives to use environmentally responsible sup-
pliers and materials to the fullest extent possible in the publishing of its
books. Such materials include vegetable-based, low-VOC inks and acid-
free papers that are recycled, totally chlorine-free, or partly composed
of nonwood fibers. For further information, visit our website at www.
cornellpress.cornell.edu.

Cloth printing   10 9 8 7 6 5 4 3 2 1
Paperback printing 10 9 8 7 6 5 4 3 2 1

Contents

Figures and Tables

Tables

ACKNOWLEDGMENTS

We have benefited greatly from discussions with many colleagues over the years. We would particularly like to thank David Leheny for giving us invaluable feedback above and beyond the call of duty.

Our sincere thanks go to the following people who provided special assistance: Sugawara Taku, who allowed us to use some material on recent House of Councillors elections from an article coauthored with Kabashima Ikuo; Gregory Noble, for thoughtful discussions and the references he suggested; Yamamoto Koji; Kanazawa Yuki for research assistance; Robin LeBlanc; Sherry L. Martin; Lee Bong Yeong; Malinda Markham; and Geoff Ng. We would also like to thank Samuel L. Popkin, James T. Hamilton, Susan Shirk, Taniguchi Masaki, and Sean Richey for comments on previous drafts of chapter 4. We are grateful to the 21st-century COE program, Invention of Policy Systems in Advanced Countries, for financial support.

Many thanks go to Roger M. Haydon, our editor at Cornell University Press, for brilliant advice. We are grateful also to the anonymous referee and to all of the team at the Press for their excellent work editing our manuscript.

Gill particularly thanks John C. Campbell, for advice and support and for being a wonderful mentor. Gill's colleagues and the administrative staff in the Social Psychology Department at the Graduate School of Humanities and Sociology, University of Tokyo, are always incredibly supportive. Her warmest thanks also go to John Williams and to her family (yes, it's the same book).

Ikuo thanks the members of the seventh Kabashima Seminar, particularly Shiraito Yuki, who shared their data and produced the book *The Koizumi Regime,* edited by the Ikuo Kabashima Seminar (Bokutakusha 2008).

We are very grateful to Matsumura Hiroshi for allowing us to reprint the LDP Promotions Derby cartoon. Some sections of chapter 4 were previously published in "How Junichiro Koizumi Seized the Leadership of Japan's Liberal Democratic Party," *Japanese Journal of Political Science* 8, no. 1 (April 2007): 95–114, copyright © 2007 Cambridge University Press, reprinted with permission. Sections of chapter 5 were originally published in "The Koizumi Revolution," *PS Political Science and Politics* 40, no. 1 (January 2007): 79–84, copyright © 2007 Cambridge University Press, reprinted with permission. The sources used for appendix A include Japan International Cooperation Agency 2008 (we thank Iizuka Keiko for facilitating this) and Abe, Shindo, and Kawato 1994.

Abbreviations

ASSK	Akarui Senkyo Suishin Kyokai (Society for the Promotion of Clean Elections)
ATES	*Asahi Shimbun*/Tokyo University Political Elite Surveys
CEFP	Council on Economic and Fiscal Policy
DPJ	Democratic Party of Japan
DSP	Democratic Socialist Party
FILP	Fiscal Investment and Loan Program
JEDS	Japan Election and Democracy Survey
JES	Japan Election Study
LDP	Liberal Democratic Party
LP	Liberal Party
JCP	Japanese Communist Party
JDP	Japan Democratic Party
JSP	Japan Socialist Party
MMD	multimember district
MoF	Ministry of Finance
NCP	New Conservative Party
NFP	New Frontier Party
PARC	Policy Affairs Research Council
PR	proportional representation
SCAP	Supreme Commander for the Allied Powers
SDPJ	Social Democratic Party of Japan
SMD	single-member district
SNTV	single nontransferable vote

NOTE ON EXCHANGE RATES

The yen exchange rate varied greatly during the postwar period. Exchange rates for various currencies, from 1950 to 2005, are provided by the Research and Statistics Department of the Bank of Japan at www.stat.go.jp/data/chouki/zuhyou/18-08.xls.

CHANGING POLITICS IN JAPAN

1

INTRODUCTION

This book is about the changes that have shaken up the Japanese political system and transformed it almost beyond recognition in the last couple of decades. We set out to demolish further the once prevalent myth that Japanese politics are a stagnant set of entrenched systems and interests that are fundamentally undemocratic. We aim to replace it with a description of a dynamic democracy, in which politicians and parties are increasingly responding to citizens' concerns and the media and other actors play a substantial role in keeping accountability alive and healthy.

In the following chapters we examine some of the most important changes in the political system, focusing particularly on the shift in the relationship between voters and officials (elected and otherwise) to show how voters either respond to or control political elites and, in turn, how officials both respond to and try to influence voters. We describe how all the political parties in Japan have adapted in how they attempt to channel votes, and we argue that, contrary to many journalistic stereotypes, the government is increasingly acting in the "the interests of citizens"—by which we mean the average voter's preferences.

Throughout the book, we return time and again to the theme of changes in *representation* and *accountability*. These are notoriously contested terms, and for those interested in a detailed theoretical discussion, Manin, Przeworski, and Stokes (1999) provide an excellent overview in their introduction to *Democracy, Accountability, and Representation*. However, our goal in this work is not to theorize about the terms but rather to track changes in political behavior, so we opt for the minimalist conceptions suggested by Ellis Krauss and Robert Pekkanen:

> By representation we mean how well and equally distributed representation is compared to the people represented; by accountability we mean how direct or distant the connection between a representative and her constituents are and whether those who represent them make policies responsive to those who elected them, as well as whether such policies respond generally to the preferences of all citizens or to narrow minorities. (2008, 11–12)

In addition, we do not assume that voters' policy preferences are necessarily exogenous or unchanging, or that voters even have preferences on every issue. Because they are highly aware of the complexity of voters' behavior, policymakers sometimes attempt to anticipate citizens' judgments when creating policies, or at other times try to mobilize the public to support their own policy agendas by framing a policy issue in a particular way. This has been the case in some areas of welfare policymaking and—most famously—in postal reform. But in some cases, these attempts have proved unsuccessful, as in failed attempts to normalize relations with North Korea or the unsuccessful campaigns to get public backing for educational reform. Overall, though, we sketch a picture of increasing accountability in a society in which citizens have more tools to judge government performance and punish or reward accordingly and the government shows increasing sensitivity to these judgments.

Voters and Parties in Postwar Politics

Analysts often divide postwar Japanese politics into four periods: 1945 to 1955, 1955 to 1993, 1993 to 2007, and 2007 to the present. During each period, changes occurred in politician-voter relations, but the changes in each period were markedly different. During the first period, a multiparty system flourished with conservative and left-wing parties competing in elections and alternating in government. Most of the governments formed during this period were either coalition or minority governments, and only one of the nine governments formed before 1955 was based on a single-party legislative majority. Politicians switched parties constantly, parties merged and collapsed with alacrity, and citizens' partisan alignment was correspondingly flexible (Yamada et al. 2008).

The LDP System

The second period began in 1955 when both the Japan Socialist Party (JSP) and the Liberal Democratic Party (LDP) formed within a short period, replacing the multiparty framework. For the next thirty-eight years, the LDP dominated politics and generally formed single-party majority governments.[1] While various other parties won a considerable share of the vote, until the 1990s none of these parties posed a serious threat to the monopoly of the LDP. Both their own actions and the electoral system marginalized the opposition parties.

As we outline in the next chapter, in the LDP system (analysts often refer to it as the "1955 system"), the relationships between ordinary voters and politicians were based on the personal ties that candidates cultivated within their own constituencies. For this reason the national government could in some ways be considered "representative," but it came to its own conclusions about what was in the best interests of the country (see Manin, Przeworski, and Stokes 1999), conclusions that largely centered on government-managed economic growth.

This was a period of growth that was export led, extensively regulated, and included protection of the domestic economy, which was costly but kept companies in business and employment levels high (see Pempel 1998). Rather than being laissez-faire capitalism, it was what T. J. Pempel (1998) has referred to as a kind of neomercantilism that amplified the connections between politics and business.[2] The standard view of the period therefore describes a pedestrian, locked-in system in which the so-called Iron Triangle of top bureaucrats in cahoots with conservative politicians and business groups controlled decision making, leaving a limited range of political action open to ordinary citizens (see, for example, Johnson 1982; Pempel 1974).

Machine politics fueled the system, and the party used all its incumbent muscle to channel public projects and financial assistance to rural areas. In turn, rural voters overwhelmingly supported the LDP, making it extremely difficult for other parties to challenge them in these constituencies. Critics derided the wasteful pork barrel public works projects that typified the system, but the construction industry, swollen from postwar reconstruction,

---

1. Both houses in Japan's bicameral parliamentary system are directly elected. Appendix A outlines the structure of the Diet for readers unfamiliar with Japan's institutions.

2. Pempel (1998) describes changes in the political economy of the period in detail.

continued to grow and sponsor the LDP political machine. A good deal of the construction industry's business was based on government contracts during this period, when "paving, erecting, and damming...became a national obsession" (Schlesinger 1997, 141). The LDP awarded contracts with little disclosure or justification, and bid-rigging and bribery became the order of the day. Politicians gained access to the money and employee votes that construction companies offered, and bureaucrats and companies sought to keep spending high. In the early 1960s, construction spending was about one fifth of Japan's GNP, and by the 1980s, it still employed 10 percent of the workforce (Schlesinger 1997, 141).

Under this system, the LDP was able to win a majority of the seats in elections for the House of Representatives until 1990, with only three exceptions (1976, 1979, and 1983). Between 1983 and 1986, the LDP entered a coalition with the New Liberal Club, a small conservative group that had broken away from the LDP in 1976. But apart from this, the LDP consistently formed single-party governments throughout these years.[3] In retrospect, these episodes look like minor exceptions to overall dominance, but at the time things were much more dramatic than they now appear, and the LDP managed to pull through by astute political maneuvering. Even during its heyday, the LDP was forced to deal with several serious crises that threatened not only its dominance but its very existence. It overcame these crises in sometimes astonishing ways—at times through astute maneuvering, at times through sheer luck.

The cliché of Japan's bubble economy, a bubble that reached its peak between 1986 and 1990, was that Japan had a first-rate economy and a third-rate government. Despite the existence of democratic institutions and the public's overwhelming support for democracy as a system, many observers view Japanese democracy during this period as substandard and inferior to other (Western) democracies. These unsatisfactory politics were tolerated when the economy was buoyant, but at the beginning of the 1990s, when the economy sank into recession, commentators began to blame the government for the state of the economy and used this as a reason not only to disparage the ruling parties for their perceived failure but to blame the political system itself.

Some see Japanese citizens as complicit in the failure of the democratic process (see Stockwin 1999), and they have labeled the system a

---

3. The New Liberal Club was tiny in comparison to the LDP, and this period can barely be described as an interruption in LDP dominance. Most members of the New Liberal Club returned to the LDP after the 1986 election.

"spectator democracy" in which uninvolved and apathetic voters do not choose parties or candidates according to policy preferences or ideological commitment but simply "deliver" their vote when requested. In response to repeated political scandals and the unpopular consumption (sales) tax, however, citizens briefly mobilized in the late 1980s, contributing to the demise of the LDP system. And though that flash of citizen activism was not sustained, voters began to distance themselves from the corrupt system as the 1990s progressed. Voting rates plummeted dramatically during the elections held in the 1990s. By 1993 only 23 percent of citizens said they were satisfied with contemporary politics, while 29 percent said that they did not support any political party at all, according to the Akarui Senkyo Suishin Kyokai (ASSK) (Society for the Promotion of Clean Elections) Lower House Election Survey 1993.

The Contemporary System

The LDP system had kept the party in power, but by the early 1990s a sense of crisis had emerged, and there was a feeling that politics as usual could not continue. As we discuss throughout this book various factors undercut the established relationships between parties and voters, leading to the declining viability of the old-style system. First, the system was obviously exploited by vested interests, and when repeated scandals revealed this, voters turned against the inherent corruption. Second, the system was financed by deficit spending that became increasingly untenable as Japan endured the prolonged recession of the 1990s. Simply put, as the economic slump continued, political leaders no longer had the resources to distribute their largesse: the pork was being sliced thin. Third, the electoral system that had contributed to the marginalization of the opposition was reformed. And fourth, citizens' expectations of party leaders and politicians changed: from the early 1990s onward leader performance rather than personal ties at the local level became increasingly important in voters' decision making, and this was augmented by increasing media coverage of politics.

As we describe in chapter 3, in 1993 the largest faction within the LDP broke into two groups, one of which eventually joined the opposition in passing a no-confidence bill against the LDP government. The LDP lost the subsequent lower house election and was replaced by a coalition government that did not include the LDP. This coalition collapsed less than a year later, but astonishingly, the LDP then managed to form a coalition with both its long-time enemy, the JSP, and Sakigake, a small party that was mainly composed of ex-LDP reformers, to establish a majority government that lasted from June 1994 to October 1996. The JSP changed its English name to Social Democratic Party of Japan in February 1991, though it continued to be called Nihon Shakaito in Japanese, and it became the Social Democratic Party (Shakai Minshuto) in January 1996. From then on, the LDP managed to continue its dominance by forming coalition governments with various smaller parties.[4]

Commentators love to evoke the bubble years in anecdotes about sushi sprinkled with gold flakes and jaw-droppingly expensive Tokyo real estate. After decades of growth in Japan, the G5 Plaza Accord in 1985 sent the yen soaring, and the Japanese government responded with monetary easing and low interest rates, which artificially pumped up real estate, stocks, and capital investment (Katz 2003). For the next few years, the bubble expanded precariously, peaking in 1989. But the massive asset-price bubble burst the following year with the simultaneous collapse of the stock market and readjustment of real estate prices, which ushered in the Heisei recession of the 1990s, an expanded national debt, a financial crisis, and a destabilized yen (Pempel 1998, 136).

Economically, the 1990s may have been a "lost decade," since none of the plans to revitalize the economy took hold, but politically, the decade was anything but lost: voter behavior changed, the parties realigned, and Japan radically transformed its systems of administration and governance. In reforming its system of governance, the crucial relationship between voters and politicians was transformed, making the system more representative.

In the coming chapters, we outline how the government became more responsive to shifts in public opinion and public demands, since it could no longer simply follow its own judgment in deciding what was best for the country as it had done during the years of the LDP system. We will show how the connection between parties and voters is shifting from the local to the national level and is increasingly tied to citizens' evaluations of government, of party leaders and politicians, and of government effectiveness. We also describe how political elites are more accountable and responsive to citizens, who now have the tools at their disposal for overseeing the actions of the political elites.

---

4. These coalitions were the LDP–Liberal Party coalition (January 1999–October 1999); the LDP–Liberal Party–Komeito coalition (October 1999–April 2000); the LDP–Komeito–Conservative Party coalition (April 2000–November 2003); and the LDP-Komeito coalition (since November 2003).

Outline of the Book

In chapter 2 we briefly describe the LDP system and how politicians and voters benefited from this system. During the period of economic growth, the LDP's "creative conservatism" incorporated a degree of responsiveness to a fairly wide range of groups, distributing enough benefits to a sufficiently broad range of people to keep them satisfied, and in return voters continued to vote for the LDP.

In chapter 3 we describe long-term trends in the vote share won by the parties, that is, who voted for each party and why. We show that whereas most voters once thought they had little choice but to select the LDP (although they voted strategically at times to force the party to remain at least somewhat responsive), they are now more willing to try the Democratic Party of Japan (DPJ). We also focus on recent trends such as the dramatic increase in independent voters and the equally dramatic way in which support for the LDP rose when the populist Koizumi Junichiro led the party, noting that when the LDP reverted to its old ways, voters were less willing to cast their vote for the old-style party. We show how a pluralistic system has emerged in which power is less concentrated and different parties have the possibility of participating in government and policymaking. The LDP has a genuine fear of being tossed out of office unlike under the old LDP system.

In chapter 4 we turn to the role of the media in changing the both the style and the substance of Japanese politics. Politicians can no longer rely on "gathering" votes through local notables, now that voters increasingly turn to the media for information and adroit politicians and political leaders are able to exploit this. Politicians have had to become media figures, and they expect to win votes as a result of media appearances. As a case study, we show how the quintessential media politician Koizumi Junichiro took advantage of changes in television news to win the 2001 LDP leadership election, and we discuss why newspapers and television were so important in this case.

In chapter 5 we look at prime ministerial popularity. When constituency-level politics was all-important in Japan, party leaders were of minimal importance to citizens' voting preferences. Now, party leaders have become important, and their popularity is crucial to party fortunes. We examine what prime ministers can do to increase their chance of survival.

In chapter 6 we look at change—and some continuity—in policies and in the policy-making process. Rather than generally being cogs in a system in which nonelected bureaucrats dominate, we show how contemporary prime ministers, who are policy entrepreneurs, are able to enact their policy agendas. We discuss the extent to which Koizumi achieved his goals and how he was able to do so, even though his reforms were outside LDP norms. We then turn to his successors and show how they have curbed the reforms and managed to pull the party back toward the old system.

In chapter 7 we turn to the Democratic Party of Japan (DPJ). For decades, the opposition parties failed to emerge as a credible alternative to the LDP, but during the 1990s, the DPJ created a two-party system at the district level and managed to seize control of the Diet's upper house in 2007 and its lower house in 2009. After briefly describing the party's history and prominent members, we examine the increasing conservative bent of the party's platform and ideology, before turning to current trends and the future of the party.

In the afterword, we briefly summarize some of the crucial changes in Japanese politics, showing how these have altered voter-party relations and speculation about the future.

2

CITIZENS AND ELITES IN THE CONSTRUCTION OF THE LDP SYSTEM

When the Allies occupied Japan from 1945 to 1952, the authorities at the general headquarters of the Supreme Commander for the Allied Powers (SCAP) enforced many sweeping political and economic reforms designed to facilitate political democracy. New Deal beliefs galvanized Occupation personnel who aimed for the demilitarization and democratization of Japan and worked zealously in every sector—political, economic, and social—to replace the old prewar systems with democratic ones. Reforms included the extension of political rights, including the rights of women to participate in politics; the legalization of the labor movement; educational reforms; land reform; and the dissolution of the *zaibatsu* (family-led industrial and financial conglomerates). The Occupation forces held war crimes tribunals and purged from public life political, administrative, and educational leaders who had advocated militarism or military nationalism (Dower 1999).

Some Japanese citizens enthusiastically responded to the expansion of their rights: they joined unions and engaged in collective bargaining and striking, joined leftist parties, demonstrated for food and better conditions, and occupied and managed their workplaces to improve conditions (Dower 1999, 254–64).

As the cold war escalated, Occupation policy reversed course to emphasize Japan's strategic importance as a capitalist ally and as a bulwark against communism. Many of the democratizing reforms that had produced an upsurge in political activity frightened the occupiers who saw them as radical, and they were jettisoned as the Americans allied more openly with the Right. Many Japanese militarists who had been purged were "depurged," and the authorities then conducted a "Red purge," firing journalists and trade union leaders whom they considered unacceptable (Dower 1999, 265–73, 433–40, 525–26).

Prime Minister Yoshida Shigeru (1946–47; 1948–54), the son of one of the young samurai reformers of the Meiji Restoration, had been raised among the "founding fathers" of modern Japan.[1] Yoshida grew up to become a diplomat and had been Japanese ambassador to Italy and then to Britain before the war. His quiet, but insistent, opposition to the war led to his arrest and several months' imprisonment in 1945 for "pro-British and American sentiments," making him the perfect ally in the eyes of the Occupation. In May 1946 he became prime minister.

Prime Minister Yoshida, as Frank Gibney puts it in the foreword to Yoshida's revised memoirs, was "immaculately turned out in his morning coat and striped trousers with wing tip collars, pince-nez spectacles and, in leisure moments, a trademark Churchillian cigar. [He] looked…like a man from another world" (2007, xii).[2] His appearance may have been anachronistic, but the policies he pushed became known as the Yoshida Doctrine and were anything but. Domestically, his administration pursued free-market policies based on Occupation directives. Internationally, he was convinced that Japan needed to ally itself with the United States. His administration signed a peace treaty that placed the country decisively in the Western bloc and concluded the United States–Japan Security Treaty to limit domestic defense forces. His friends and enemies referred to him as "One-man" for his dictatorial style and unwillingness to suffer the many people he considered fools.

Opposing these policies—having returned to public life when the purge of militarists from public life was rescinded—were people such as Kishi Nobusuke and Hatoyama Ichiro. Hatoyama reorganized the Liberal Party at the end of the war and was originally touted to be prime minister, but he was then purged by SCAP for his alleged cooperation with the military governments during the 1930s and 1940s, allowing Yoshida to gain the premiership. Hatoyama reentered politics only after being depurged. He called for Japanese autonomy and complete independence from the United States.

1. Japan's modernizing period began in earnest in 1868. The Meiji leaders ousted the Tokugawa government and enacted enormous political, social, and economic change.

2. Excerpts from Yoshida's memoirs were translated and published in English in 1961 as *The Yoshida Memoirs: The Story of Japan in Crisis.*

Kishi was one of the top officials who promoted the industrial development of Japanese-occupied Manchuria and China, and when he returned to Japan in 1940, he contributed to wartime economic organization as vice minister of commerce and industry. He spent three years in Sugamo prison under investigation as a class A war criminal (a classification that denotes committing a crime against peace, in short, waging a war of aggression), but he was not tried.[3] He and his group pushed to amend the peace clause of the Japanese Constitution and to rearm. In 1954 Kishi and his faction, Hatoyama, and some other conservatives united to form the Japan Democratic Party (JDP), which toppled the Yoshida government.

Citizens and Parties in the LDP System

The formation of the Japan Socialist Party (JSP) in 1955 put pressure on the two conservative parties, Yoshida's Liberal Party and the Japan Democratic Party, to merge in order to counter the strength of the socialists in the Diet. A few months later these two groups merged to form the Liberal Democratic Party (LDP).

Opposing the conservatives, the Japan Socialist Party and the Japanese Communist Party supported the democratic reforms of the early Occupation. We present the creation and dissolution of postwar political parties graphically in figure 2.1.

Political leaders and citizens fought over the overall policy profile of the state. Domestically, the administrations of Kishi Nobusuke (1957–60), who was part of the Japan Democratic Party when it merged with the LDP in 1955, pushed to strengthen law and order, and Kishi himself worked relentlessly to gain political support for Constitutional revision so that Japan could rearm, become an equal security partner of the United States, and enjoy an autonomous foreign policy. His pledges to introduce universal

3. Some observers refer to Kishi as "America's favorite war criminal." As Richard Samuels (2000) points out, even in the cold war world of cynical opportunism and rapidly shifting alliances, Kishi's rehabilitation was remarkable. Kishi had been a close deputy of General Tojo for nearly a decade. Yet in June 1957, Vice President Richard Nixon introduced Prime Minister Kishi to the U.S. Senate as an "honored guest" who was "not only a great leader of the free world, but also a loyal and great friend of the people of the United States." On that trip, Kishi also threw the first pitch at a New York Yankees baseball game and played golf with President Eisenhower in an otherwise racially segregated country club (see Samuels 2000).

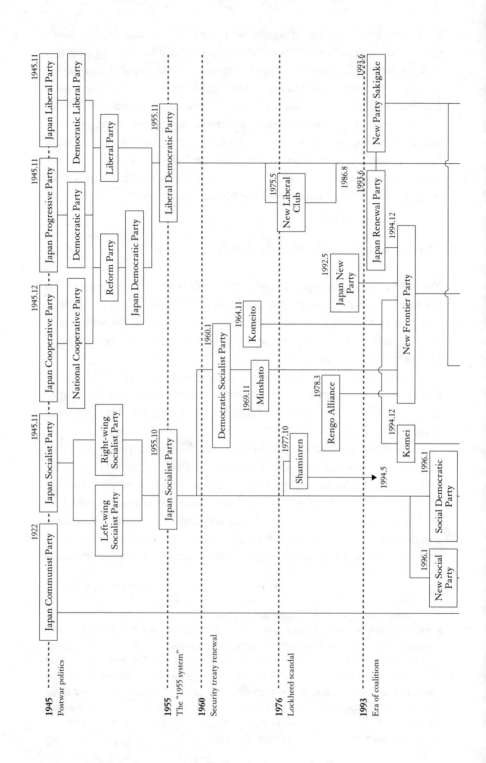

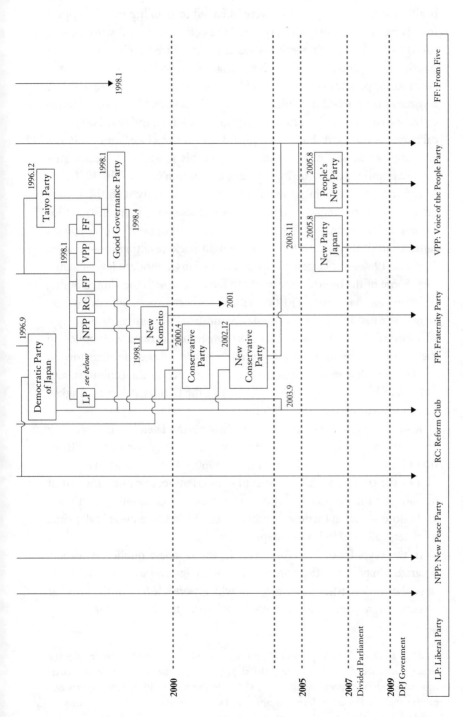

Figure 2.1. The evolution of parties in postwar Japan. Based on *Asahi Contemporary Terms* [*Asahi gendai yogo chiezo*] (2005).

LP: Liberal Party   NPP: New Peace Party   RC: Reform Club   FP: Fraternity Party   VPP: Voice of the People Party   FF: From Five health insurance and pensions were intended to mobilize public support for his party. Kishi allegedly exploited the collection and distribution of funds to the fullest, pioneering a system that utilized various sources of political funds and instigating what Richard J. Samuels (2001) describes as "the most sophisticated money laundering operation in Japanese politics," a system that reached its zenith under Tanaka Kakuei (1972–74). Specifically, Kishi used American funds and public resources, and relied on political fixers with alleged shady underworld connections (see Samuels 2001). Although Kishi was not formally charged, his fund-raising techniques were part and parcel of the high-profile corruption cases of the 1950s.

Internationally, Kishi signed a revised security treaty with the United States in 1960, provoking a major political crisis. Many journalists, opposition parties, unions, intellectuals, and grassroots organizations opposed ratification of the revised treaty and fought back, resulting in—between 1959 and 1960—the largest mass demonstrations in modern Japanese history. Some of the opposition sought to loosen ties with the United States, others would have preferred ties with the Soviet Union, and still others were disturbed by the lack of debate. Hundreds of thousands of people surrounded the Diet in June 1960. Demonstrators clashed with police on the steps of the building (some protestors expressed their feelings toward the treaty with a mass urination on the entrance to the building), and politicians physically fought on the floor of the Diet itself (for an English language account, see *Time* 1960).[4]

Kishi managed to get the revision through the Diet, but the backlash was so strong that he was forced to resign. Kishi's successor, former Ministry of Finance bureaucrat Ikeda Hayato (1960–64), tried to avoid a repetition of the conflict with his low-profile international posture. Instead of focusing on international relations, he focused on economic growth and his famous National Income-Doubling Plan. Most subsequent LDP prime ministers followed in his footsteps.

In the years following World War II, the Japanese public was deeply polarized, in part over their preferences on foreign and security policy and in part over domestic issues, many of which were a legacy of the postwar Occupation reforms. The party system mirrored the divisions for decades,

---

4. In a failed effort to prevent Kishi's departure to the United States to sign the treaty, hundreds of protesters seized the airport building the night before his departure, wrecked the airport's restaurant, and fought the police with bamboo spears and pepper shakers. Protesters lined the approaches to the airport, but Kishi managed to avoid what he called the "distasteful, insignificant demonstration" (*Time* 1960).

but the majority of the voting public then, and for many years thereafter, supported the merged conservative parties, ensuring the conservatives' long-term control of the government. The LDP also indirectly served the industrial, commercial, and farm interests of their major supporters. The JSP and other opposition parties continued to voice strong resistance, and a substantial minority of voters supported these parties. These parties were able to marshal the support of the trade union movement and appeal to popular apprehension about the fragility of peace and the new democratic reforms.

Ideologically, the 1955 system was based on competition between the JSP and the LDP and manifested itself in the cleavage that most divided the electorate, pitting the leftist defenders of Japan's postwar pacifist Constitution against the conservative defenders of the 1960 U.S.-Japan Security Treaty (known in Japan as Anpo, a contraction of the Japanese term). Although the cleavage weakened over time, a voter's stance on the security treaty issue remained the single best predictor of his or her vote as late as 1976 (Flanagan 1991b, 117).

Relations among politicians and between politicians and voters both shaped, and were shaped by, the LDP. Leaders of the parties that had merged to form the LDP struggled for power in the new party. Party leaders began organizing their followers into exclusive factions to help their leader become party president, and thus prime minister (Thayer 1969, 6–24). In return, followers gained access to party and government posts— which became the objects of factional bargaining—and help in gaining the party's endorsement and funding. Commentators have criticized factions as weakening the party and its image by breeding corruption and financial dependence on big business, since faction leaders needed lots of money to distribute to faction members to ensure their reelection, and undermining the power and stability of the prime minister's office (Krauss 1989, 47). Over the years, faction leaders and party members resisted efforts to reform or abolish factions.

The electoral system for the House of Representatives from 1947 to 1993 made access to funds particularly important (see Krauss and Pekkanen 2008, 13–14). Japan had a relatively unusual multimember district (MMD) system in which voters cast a single nontransferable vote (SNTV). In each district, three to five candidates (later two to six in select districts) were elected. Thus, an LDP candidate's main rivals were often not opposition parties' candidates but other LDP candidates running in the same district. Strict election campaigning rules limited candidates' contact with voters except during the short period prior to the election. They strongly limited advertising, leaving candidates few ways to mobilize votes—although in practice, candidates found ways around some of these rules.

The flaws of the system are well known: since more than one candidate from the same party ran in any given district, the LDP could not aid any one of its multiple candidates more than any other in a given district, so LDP candidates had to find their own strategies for reaching voters. They did so by cultivating a personal vote because it did not make sense for candidates to attempt to distinguish themselves from their opponents on the basis of policies, party label, or ideology, as some of their opponents were from exactly the same party. The personal support networks—*koenkai*—tended to emphasize local, rather than national, issues and were private "clubs" that provided social opportunities for members. They allowed politicians to reach their followers outside the campaign period and to be responsive to constituents, often by bringing pork barrel projects to the district as well as assistance of all kinds (Kabashima 2004; Kobayashi 1991; Krauss and Pekkanen 2008; Schlesinger 1997). In return, *koenkai* members were expected to turn out to vote and to mobilize others in their networks to do so. Given that it often required only 15–20 percent of the vote in a district to place among the winners in that district, concentrating on personal networks was often enough to ensure electoral success.

Analysts blamed the electoral system for many of the ills in Japanese politics, particularly the money-based nature of politics and the lack of focus on policy issues (Otake 1998). The *koenkai* cost a fortune to maintain, and faction leaders and individual LDP Diet members were constantly attempting to raise money from business interests, both local and national, to fund these organizations and their election campaigns. A Diet member's annual salary was 19 million yen (the exchange rate at the time was around 138 yen per U.S. dollar), which led to a huge discrepancy between members' official incomes and their expenditures: they were expected to attend important events in their constituents' lives and to provide the customary monetary gifts. Jacob Schlesinger quotes a survey from 1989 of one hundred Diet members. Each attended an average of 6.6 weddings and 26.5 funerals per month, costing an individual politician a total of 550,000 yen in gifts. "During the New Year's season, an MP would be expected to keep up with the breathless pace of attending thirty parties a day, shelling out 600,000 yen a month. And no sector of society was above demanding help with emergencies" (Schlesinger 1997, 225). The price of winning a seat in the Diet in the 1980s had spiraled to around 500 million yen, and an incumbent Diet member's nonelection year expenses ran to 100 million yen (Schlesinger 1997, 224–25).

Commentators pointed to candidate-based support systems (and the fundraising and distribution of pork that was part of this system) as a major cause of corruption, as many representatives relied on contributions to offset the exorbitant costs of election campaigns. Typical LDP politicians channeled financial aid from the government to the rural areas they represented and received campaign contributions in return. Others went further and participated in the bid-rigging and massive bribery that characterized the system.

In addition to developing *koenkai,* some LDP politicians began to develop expertise in specific policy areas to differentiate themselves from LDP rivals running in the same district. Those who were successful joined and rose to executive positions in the party's Policy Affairs Research Council (PARC, the main policymaking organ within the party, the committees of which are organized in parallel to the ministries), Diet committees, the subcabinet, and eventually cabinet posts in that area. Politicians who specialize in a specific policy area or *seisaku zoku* ("policy tribe") develop relationships with bureaucrats and can greatly influence policymaking (Ramseyer and Rosenbluth 1994, 31–34; Krauss and Pekkanen 2008).

Growth, Stability, and Income Equality

Although the system became mired in corruption, ordinary citizens still reaped immense—almost unimaginable—benefits from it. At the end of the war, Japan was in ruins—around 2.7 million servicemen had died in the war, many millions more people were malnourished, wounded, or sick. Two thirds of the major cities had been heavily bombed, leaving them mostly flattened and millions of people homeless. For years afterward, people crowded into shantytowns, barely able to make ends meet, lacking food, while any money they had became worthless as postwar inflation spiraled (Dower 1999, 45–61).

Incredibly, within a few short years, Japan picked itself up, and the LDP government was able to lead the country back to prosperity. Efficient policymaking contributed to the rapid economic growth of postwar Japan—often referred to as an "economic miracle." This outcome was at variance with the dominant theories of development at the time (Huntington and Nelson, 1976; Kuznets 1963). Japan pursued a model of political and economic development in which citizens experienced the benefits of economic growth while enjoying income egalitarianism and a stable democracy (Kabashima 1984). Citizens benefited from a higher

standard of living, low unemployment, and low inflation during Japan's
four decades of unprecedented growth (Pempel 1998).[5]

This is not to say that Japan has been an ideal democracy. The LDP
has managed to maintain power through a wide variety of means, both
fair and questionable. From mid-1997 the LDP maintained power as the
dominant partner in coalition governments, and politicians have been involved in several massive and notorious corruption scandals. However,
elections are regular, free, and open, and voters have used the ballot in
strategic ways to achieve policy change. Even during its heyday, the LDP
had to be somewhat responsive to public opinion, enacting policies the
public favored when it absolutely had to in order to win votes that might
otherwise have gone to the opposition parties (although the electoral system contributed to the marginalization of the opposition).

The farmers and middle class provided the LDP with a consistent man-
date that allowed it the freedom to pursue its economic policy agenda.
Farmers and small shopkeepers disproportionately turned out to vote,
and they overwhelmingly voted for the LDP—a vote that was magnified
by the malapportionment that we discuss in chapter 3. In return for this
"supportive participation" as crucial pillars of the LDP, farmers and small
businesses received patronage in the form of protection from imports and
urban-based large firms.[6]

This broad-based, supportive participation admittedly does not fit
the citizen-based "town meeting" ideal of democracy. However, the LDP
system redistributed national wealth to rural districts, thus minimizing
rural-urban income disparities and helping preserve the democratic system. It softened the divisive tension among social groups and moderated
demands for radical change that accompanied rapid economic development, even while becoming a breeding ground for corruption.

Scheiner (2005) argues convincingly that besides the corruption inherent in the centralized, clientelistic state, the nature of the state contributes
to opposition failure in Japan. The regions and prefectures are clients of
the centralized state; opposition failure is not only the electoral failure
of the opposition to take control at the national level but, importantly, a
problem of the local level. Local-level politicians need connections to the

---

5. After a readjustment period following the oil shocks, Japan's economy continued to grow, albeit at a slower rate.

6. Pempel (1998) describes in detail the mutually reinforcing relationships within
the dominant socioeconomic coalition, the major political-economic institutions, and
the profile of public policy during this period.

national government to secure subsidies, and thus local-level politicians who have connections to LDP Diet members do well in local elections. Failure at the local level has contributed to national-level opposition failure by depriving opposition parties of "quality" candidates, that is, candidates with previous experience. Although variance across prefectures does exist, Scheiner points out that rural districts are the most prone to this kind of clientelism that contributes to local-national failure, which in turn is compounded by the fact that there are more rural than urban districts.

Although some analysts refer to the Japanese system as "socialist," the wealth redistribution that took place during the economy's period of high growth was largely in the form of farm subsidies and massive public works projects. Unlike state spending in the Soviet Union or the welfare states of Scandinavia, the Japanese central government deliberately kept its spending on social provision small, mainly providing pensions and health insurance for the elderly, with comparatively meager provisions for the unemployed, single mothers, and children. Instead, companies and families (particularly women) provided benefits and care (see Schoppa 2006, 36–65).

Policymaking: Bureaucrats, Politicians, and Citizens

A further significant characteristic of the postwar system in Japan has been the influence of the national bureaucracy, especially the economic ministries, which facilitated growth through their role in policymaking. Crucially, the bureaucracy was permeable enough to allow politics to shape development in an egalitarian direction. Although big business pushed the formation of the LDP, the party was also supported by former bureaucrats; this combination led to government-managed industrial policies, tight fiscal policies, rapid technological improvement of large firms, protectionism, and export-led expansion. (See Pempel 1998 and Katz 1998 for detailed descriptions.)

Yet, as scholars frequently note, the relations among bureaucrats and politicians are not straightforward. John C. Campbell, a longtime expert on policymaking, bluntly commented, "Democracy and bureaucracy are fundamentally antithetical. Democracy is bottom-up political process devoted to responsiveness. Bureaucracy is top-down administrative structure devoted to rationality" (Campbell 1989, 113). In Japan, as in other democracies, the two conflicting normative goals of effective policymaking and democratic responsiveness sometimes clash, although they are harmonious at other times. As long as the bureaucracy and the LDP shared similar goals, the LDP had no need to confront the bureaucracy or to seek policy-relevent expertise from outside the bureaucracy. As professor of political science at Columbia University and long-standing expert on Japanese politics, Gerald L. Curtis, points out, the bureaucracy retained a great deal of authority because it did not challenge the overall policy profile of the state. Although at times bureaucrats were able to sabotage particular policies, they were careful not to publicly challenge the LDP (1999, 229).

The "normal" LDP approach to policymaking is a decentralized, bottom-up affair both in the LDP and in the ministries. The rare entrepreneurial prime ministers did give policy direction but left the details to the bureaucrats. The process involves *zoku giin,* politicians who specialize in a specific policy area, bureaucrats with whom they can develop close and mutually beneficial relationships, and, increasingly, citizens (Campbell 1989, 122–34). All wield influence over policymaking. On the LDP side, the *zoku* are involved in the discussions in the Policy Affairs Research Council, the subcommittees, and the Diet committees (Sato and Matsuzaki 1986; Ramseyer and Rosenbluth 1994). The PARC used to have seventeen subcommittees (later reduced to thirteen) and over thirty research commissions. The subcommittees were the first discussion forum in discussions of government-proposed policy. If a subcommittee approved a proposal (after any amendments), the proposal was then sent to the PARC, and finally to the LDP General Council, where the decision had to be unanimous (Shinoda 2007, 24). The *zoku giin* could veto policies at each stage of the process.

On the ministry side, the main working-level officers are deputy directors (*kacho hosa*) in their late thirties and early forties who discuss their own policy proposals within the section. If the proposal is approved, it is then brought to a working-level meeting with other sections within the same bureau. If the other sections approve, the proposal is finalized as a bureau decision with the approval of the bureau's directors, after coordinating with officials in other ministry bureaus and after legal and budget examinations (see Shinoda 2007, 23–25).

Analysts debate the question of who actually dominates policymaking in Japan. Some argue that the nonelected career bureaucrats create policies that the elected politicans merely rubber-stamp and that the role of citizens in this process is negligible. Some commentators criticize this as undemocratic, but this process accords with the notion of democracy as officials making policy in the national interest and in a highly efficient manner, rather than making policies that are responsive to small shifts in public opinion (Huber and Powell 1994).

In practice, politicians have not been simply rubber-stampers. The bureaucracy is certainly an elite that has at times held sway in some areas of policymaking, but as Campbell has pointed out, no single ministry is able to dominate decision making, interministerial turf battles have been increasing, and top-down policymaking has been on the rise for some time (Campbell, 1989, 122–23). Furthermore, since a basic consensus was established on the overall public-policy profile of the state, that is, a profile that prioritized rapid economic growth and a low posture internationally, fundamental conflict over policies was blunted to some extent.

A series of studies by Japanese scholars during the 1980s contended that a major shift had occurred: whereas once bureaucrats dominated, the LDP rank and file had taken on a much larger role in the policy-making process. Campbell and Scheiner (2008) review some of the studies and conclude that under the LDP system, bureaucrats and politicians usually cooperated in policymaking. More precisely, as Campbell and Scheiner note, "focusing on competition between politicians and bureaucrats creates an impression of two wholly distinct groups, when very often *alliances* of politicians and bureaucrats battle other alliances of politicians and bureaucrats" (2008, 90). Because many LDP politicians were former bureaucrats these alliances were particularly strong.

Constraints on Leadership

The prime minister has typically exercised little direct control over policy, and while some commentators think that bureaucrats make effective policy, others prefer stronger prime ministerial direction in policymaking. Shimizu Masato (2005), for example, in *Cabinet Leadership: Koizumi Junichiro's Revolution* (*Kantei shudo: Koizumi Junichiro no kakumei*), argues that the system is necessarily and inevitably moving toward cabinet leadership with a strong prime minister (due to various structural changes), though this has not been fully achieved. A strong prime minister who leads in policymaking may also increase the development of issue-based politics and alternation in power of contending parties. In systems where power is diffuse, if citizens are dissatisfied, it is not clear where ultimate responsibility lies: Is it with the governing party? the bureaucracy? the prime minister? The lack of clarity means that prime ministers are not blamed (or rewarded) for policy choice.

Pundits who argue that the prime minister should have a stronger hand in policymaking typically point to the structural weaknesses of the Cabinet Office (the *Kantei*) under the LDP. Narita Norihiko and Eda Kenji, former executive secretaries to prime ministers Hosokawa Morihiro (1993–94) and Hashimoto Ryutaro (1996–98), discuss the shortcomings of the Cabinet Office in an April 2002 article, "How the Prime Minister Is Kept from Leading," printed in *Ronza*, a monthly magazine published by the Asahi newspaper company, and reprinted in the *Japan Echo*, a bi-monthly journal. They argue that the Cabinet Office is understaffed and most who work there are on loan from other ministries or agencies, to which they owe their primary loyalty. In short, the prime minister has no permanent Cabinet Office staff, and he does not even have a staff that he himself can appoint. Patronage appointments are comparatively few, and of the appointments the prime minister can actually make, most are se-verely limited by party and political constraints. Narita argues that the only person a prime minister can choose freely is his personal executive secretary—the prime minister is forced to bow to party and political con-straints in appointing the chief cabinet secretary and other senior staff members (Narita and Eda 2002, 15).

Narita and Eda (2002) agree that to function effectively the prime min-ister needs to have his own team of loyal advisers. Both see bureaucrats as the strongest source of resistance to the reform efforts of the prime ministers for whom they worked. They believe that the bureaucrats were able to resist reform because the prime minister's executive office did not function as it should, noting how it fell short of the arrangements in other countries. In the United States the president has a staff of advisers within the White House; in France and Germany the leaders also enjoy policy support within their offices. In Japan, at the time they wrote, only about thirty policy staff worked in the Cabinet Office; policymaking was out-sourced to the ministries in Kasumigaseki, the ward in Tokyo where most of the bureaucrcy is located. As Narita and Eda put it, "In a nutshell, the bureaucracy is dictating the nation's policies by using the prime minister as its mouthpiece."

Reforming the System

Yet some prime ministers did embark on major policy shifts. Faced with the limitations of their office, reformist leaders were able to achieve their objectives through deliberately reforming the entire administrative system, strengthening the Cabinet Office, establishing and creatively using advisory councils, and using public support as leverage.

Administrative Reform

A series of laws enacted by the administrations of Nakasone Yasuhiro (1982–87), Hashimoto Ryutaro (1996–98), and Koizumi Junichiro (2001–06) reformed the overall system of administration and practice of governance. As Kume Ikuo points out, the term "administrative reform" is misleading and actually describes packages of policies with a common ideology of laissez-faire liberalism: "Small government, deregulation, and privatization," in principle, a neoconservative package similar to those of the Thatcher and Reagan administrations (Kume 1996, 222). But in Japan, none of the reformist prime ministers presented a coherent, consistent neoliberal ideology, but rather they concentrated on pet projects and left alone some potentially politically treacherous areas (see Noble 2005, 3), producing a piecemeal approach to change. Japan moved toward neoliberalism in some areas, while leaving untouched other areas, such as those that might increase unemployment (Noble 2005).

Nakasone built on the administrative reforms initiated by the Suzuki administration and tried to radically change the policy profile in what he described as a "comprehensive restructuring of the postwar political regime" [*sengo seiji no sokessan*] (see Muramatsu and Kume 1988). Some analysts see the Nakasone reforms as one element in a series of reforms that continued into the 1990s and 2000s that sought to reduce the size and influence of government. (For details of the Nakasone reforms see, for example, Kawabata 2008, Johnson 1989, and Vogel 1996.) The LDP system honed by Prime Minister Tanaka Kakuei (1972–74)—who famously "never saw a spending program he didn't like"—was proving too expensive. Some bureaucrats attempted to control spending, but they were ineffective in the face of politicians' demands for high public spending. From the mid-1960s, the government had abandoned its balanced budget policy and began relying on bonds to finance its expenditures. The oil crisis in 1973 put an end to expectations of continued dramatic growth and coincided with what became known as "Japan's first year of high social welfare." With slower growth and lower tax revenues, the government increasingly turned to deficit spending rather than risk unpopular tax increases (see Pempel 1998, 188).

Fiscal austerity flew in the face of what had become politicians' standard operating procedure: the ability to channel public projects to their constituencies and reap the benefits—votes and funds—that this brought. As Japan descended more deeply into government debt and had to issue more bonds to service its existing debt, the government and the Ministry of Finance proposed introducing a consumption (sales) tax to reduce the red ink, a proposal that resulted in a resounding defeat for the party in the 1979 lower house election. By the early 1980s, an alliance of reformist politicians, led by Nakasone and supported by business leaders who were worried about tax increases, mounted what John Campbell described as a campaign for fiscal tightening (Campbell 1989, 127–28). Reformers framed the campaign as preventing a "bloated bureaucracy" from expanding the functions of government. Under the banner of "financial reconstruction without tax increases," reformers mobilized public opinion, big business groups (in contrast to their demands for more spending during the 1970s, their support came from a desire to avoid planned tax increases), and private-sector unions (Kume 1996, 223). As a result, public support for the Nakasone cabinet increased.

Nakasone set the basic pattern of government reform in which the prime minister exercises leadership with support from his knowledgeable staff and leaves the details to the bureaucrats (Kawabata 2008). Nakasone privatized major government corporations, such as Nippon Telephone and Telegraph and the Japanese National Railways, and deregulated the telecommunications market. He also tried to delegate more responsibility for provision of social services to the private sphere. The government tried to reduce its functions and budget expenditure; the ratio of the budget to GNP decreased in 1984 for the first time since 1973, and a policy of no increases was implemented for five years (Kume 1996, 222). As part of the latter process, welfare cuts were enacted, unconditional free medical services for the elderly were ended, and pension benefits were lowered (see Campbell 1992). We discuss the Hashimoto reforms in chapter 6.

Advisory Councils

Prime Ministers who were policy entrepreneurs—Nakasone, Hosokawa, Hashimoto, and Koizumi—all used councils, commissions, and policy aides to provide ideological justification and expertise in their reform drives and to strengthen their respective positions in the policy-making process. As the director general of the Administrative Management Agency (and later prime minister) in Suzuki Zenko's administration in the early 1980s, Nakasone established the Ad Hoc Commission for Administrative Reform (Rinji Gyosei Chosakai, or Rincho, for short) in March 1981 (see Pempel 1998, 189–90). With support from Prime Minister Suzuki, Rincho submitted five reports recommending various reforms, including spending cuts, administrative reform, and the privatization of some government-owned industries (Ishi 1993, 320–21). Rincho's recommendations also prompted the creation of the Management and Coordination Agency by merging the Administrative Management Agency with the Prime Minister's Office in order to give the prime minister greater powers to oversee the bureaucracy (Kawabata 2008).

When Nakasone succeeded Suzuki as prime minister, he continued to pursue reform by pushing Rincho recommendations through the legislative process (Kawabata 2008, 254–56). Nakasone talked explicitly about "top-down policymaking," and to bring this about he convened high-profile advisory committees to counter any Diet or bureaucratic resistence and to provide advice on controversial neoliberal projects (Shinoda 2004).

Public Opinion

Public support for reform is often crucial in bringing it about. Powerful LDP factions and bureaucrats opposed each of the major prime minister–led reforms, and the antireformers forced the reformers into negotiations and dramatic political showdowns (see Kawabata 2008; Noble 2005). Each of the reforms was eventually framed as a solution to citizen dissatisfaction, and gaining public support provided the reformists the leverage they needed to push through their policies.

Of course, it is not always possible to get the public behind reform. In the early 1980s, for example, some conservative policymakers tried to get the public to support reductions in state provision of welfare services. They framed the welfare state as cold and uncaring, essentially "un-Japanese," and instead promoted what they called a "Japanese-style welfare society," by which they meant unpaid care provided by the family (usually women) or by firms, rather than by the government. The public did not get behind these plans, which were quickly rejected as unrealistic (Campbell, J. 1992).

Another axis of conservative-progressive confrontation emerged during the late 1960s and early 1970s. Citizen activism surged as the undesirable by-products of rapid economic growth—pollution and environmental damage—could no longer be ignored. The socialists pushed for environmental protection measures as well as for expansion of social welfare programs. After winning several local elections, the progressives began implementing tremendously popular welfare programs. These policies were eventually co-opted by the LDP when faced with electoral pressure. This political flexibility or "creative conservatism," to use T. J. Pempel's (1982) phrase, averted an LDP-versus-opposition policy cleavage that might have caused voters to punish the governing LDP at the polls. At that time, social services, including nursing homes and in-home care, were still means-tested and not usually available to anyone who could be cared for in the family (Campbell and Ikegami 2000). The state began introducing programs for older people in 1963, but the first major expansion was not until 1973, when medical care was made virtually free for people seventy and older (and the bedridden age sixty-five and older).

Similarly, public support—or the necessity of drumming up votes—influenced the introduction of some major new programs in 1990. A series of scandals, flanked by the introduction of the unpopular consumption (sales) tax in 1989 during the administration of Takeshita Noboru, angered voters and led to significant losses for the LDP in the 1989 House of Councillors election (see chapter 3). In response, and faced with an upcoming lower house election, Hashimoto Ryutaro, a longtime welfare policy expert, committed the government to expanding welfare programs. Against the background of Japan's much-publicized rapidly aging population and with the decline of families' capacity to provide in-home care, the LDP came up with its Ten-Year Strategy to Promote Health and Welfare for the Aged (informally known as the Gold Plan) in December 1989 as its major campaign promise for the lower house election early the next year. In enacting these pledges, the government took on a big new responsibility to provide long-term care to all frail older people, not just the poor or those without families. Public demand for services exceeded all expectations, and the programs were later expanded in the New Gold Plan. This was a surprising commitment, given the calls for budget restraint and Japan's economic slump.[7]

Margarita Estavez-Abe (2009) argues that welfare and health care reforms were enacted during the 1990s because the electoral system transformed political dynamics, forcing politicians to broaden their support base. Under the new system, it was no longer feasible to rely only on key supporters like the Medical Association and the elderly, so the LDP had to broaden its support base (the reforms were also enacted because of the political skills of Koizumi Junichiro when he was prime minister). In

---

7. Campbell and Ikegami (2000) argue that during the negotiations, cost issues were not a priority because decision makers underestimated the demand for the services.

the institutional context in which politicians had to appeal to a greater segment of the population, Japan's health care system was reformed, the government extended some benefits and services for the working-age population, and expanded unemployment benefits to cover some irregular workers, as well as policies that help mothers balance work and family, were promoted.

As John C. Campbell described it, citizens still sometimes went to bureaucrats cap in hand and risked being rejected as egotistical by haughty bureaucrats. But in addition to the "citizen as supplicant" mode of behavior, citizens had become much more assertive, and bureaucrats were forced to engage with citizens' movements and to consult with local interests on projects, as well as sometimes buying off or co-opting the opposition (Campbell 1989, 123–24). A decade later Curtis noted "the power of interest groups, and of public pressure exercised through citizen movements and elections, to force the state to adopt policies that government officials thought were unwise, and to thwart government efforts to adopt policies that the public thought were undesirable" (Curtis 1999, 229). Citizens make their demands heard through protest politics, in grassroots activities, and through participation in the advisory councils. In addition, citizens' participation has expanded dramatically since the enactment of the Special Nonprofit Organization Law (NPO law) that promotes the development of independent NPOs by liberalizing the conditions under which groups can form and operate, free from bureaucratic control. The impact of the NPO law is stronger at the local level than at the national level (see Kawato and Pekkanen 2008) since the main purpose of the law was to increase the number of NPOs that support the state's provision of services at the local level.

3

PARTY AND VOTER DEALIGNMENT

THE LDP SYSTEM DISINTEGRATES

Even a brief glance at the electoral returns in postwar Japan shows three striking trends, each of which encompasses profound changes in voter-party relations. The first of these is the LDP's dominance itself. In hindsight, commentators tend to take citizens' allegiance to the LDP for granted; after all, the party managed to dominate politics for most of the postwar period. But the LDP has faced several serious crises, during which it looked as if it would not even survive. The party did manage to pull through these crises, sometimes through adroit decision making and sometimes through sheer luck.

Second, citizens largely rejected the opposition parties, which failed to mount a credible challenge. Despite their occasional electoral success, opposition parties remained fragmented and were unwilling or unable to package themselves into an attractive unified opposition to the LDP. Over the long term, though, most opposition parties became more responsive to voters, becoming more moderate ideologically and closer to the median voter, but this was a very gradual process. Since the beginning of the twenty-first century, the Democratic Party of Japan has proved to be a credible challenge to the LDP.

Third, citizens' alignment with parties is slowly eroding: the number of independents—citizens who do not feel attached to a particular party—continues to grow, making electoral outcomes increasingly unpredictable and the traditional patterns of mobilizing a less reliable way to ensure electoral success.

Despite the LDP's dominance, a long-term electoral dealignment is taking place. The transitory effects of the rise and collapse of new parties during the 1990s did not end up creating a fundamental shift in the structure of the party system and the loyalties of voters.

What we do see in Japan—which some scholars claim is also the case in the United States—are slow movements that take place over decades (Carmines and Stimson 1989). Overall, long-term voter realignment, strengthened by ecological replacement as the younger generation replaces the older generation of more loyal LDP voters, in combination with the new electoral system is producing changes both in the connections between voters and politicians and in electoral returns. A slow process is underway in which old loyalties (and the incentives of the old system) are still evident, while movements toward new alignments have emerged, although they do not influence all voters in the same way.

LDP Dominance

Japan's postwar industrial growth caused revolutionary social and economic change that profoundly influenced citizens' values. Cross-cutting pressures resulting from urbanization and the loosening of community ties along with growing affluence make the LDP's long-term dominance all the more astounding. That being said, other factors, such as the LDP's solid organization and malapportionment, contributed to the party's electoral success. In addition they were helped by the decline of the unions and, by default, the behavior of the opposition parties.

Urbanization

In general, farmers and rural communities more solidly supported the LDP than did others. In return for their crucial support, farmers benefited from various kinds of patronage, including favorable taxes, protection from imports, and pork barrel projects. There has been massive internal migration to the cities from the countryside and concomitant decline of village populations of various sizes (see figures 3.1 and 3.2). The number of farming families decreased from 34 million households in 1946 to under 10 million in 2002, desperately shrinking the LDP's support base.

Cross-national research notes the importance of community integration in political decision making (Verba and Nie 1972, 229–46). These links are especially important in Japan in that some researchers believe

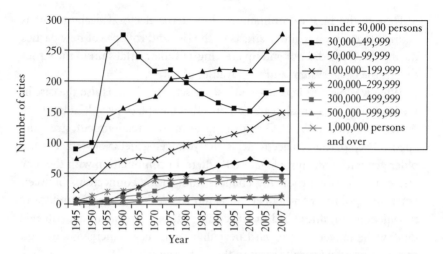

Figure 3.1. The urban population grows (number of cities and towns by size of population), 1945–2007. Data for figures 3.1 and 3.2 are based on the Population Census (October 1). Each ku area of Tokyo-to is counted as one city. Due to the amalgamation of towns and villages and to the birth of new cities under the Town and Village Merger Acceleration Law, figures for 1960 are different from those for previous years. Local Administration Bureau; Statistical Survey Department and Statistics Bureau, Ministry of Internal Affairs and Communications.

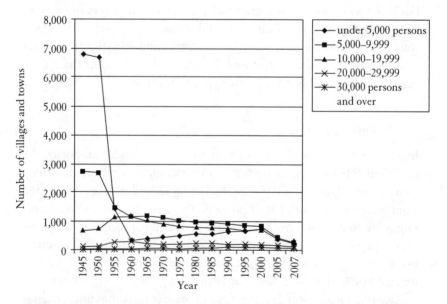

Figure 3.2. The rural population shrinks (number of villages by size of population), 1945–2007. Local Administration Bureau; Statistical Survey Department and Statistics Bureau, Ministry of Internal Affairs and Communications.

that mobilization is the determinant of vote share,[1] with the implicit assumption that a high level of community integration facilitates mobilization: local notables deliver votes to their favored politician by mobilizing their networks.[2] Following the classic studies of the 1950s and 1960s, numerous qualitative studies in Japan highlight the importance of this type of mobilization in the political process. Some subsequent research questions this received wisdom and argues that a more complex pattern of mobilization exists (Flanagan 1991b), particularly in light of the massive postwar social and economic transformation.

Typically, as communities grow, the social and economic connections that have bound people together decline. As people in Japan moved to the cities, found work in companies, experienced new lifestyles, and came into contact with new ideas, they were less likely to be integrated into community life than they had been as long-term residents in villages. Importantly, in Japan community life may include participating in community- and employment-based networks that usually support the LDP. As the rural population declined, not only were there fewer people for the LDP to mobilize, but as villages or towns amalgamated, the remaining people were harder to reach.

At the polls, the conservative parties dominated during the early postwar period, and they continued to do so after the creation of the JSP and the LDP in 1955, when the LDP gained a whopping 58 percent of the votes cast in the lower house election, as opposed to the JSP's 33 percent (see figure 3.3). The LDP vote share declined throughout the 1960s and 1970s and had fallen to 42 percent by the 1976 election. These patterns correlate with the decline in rural population, the LDP's "natural" constituency. But although demographic shifts are important in influencing a voter's choice, they do not wholly determine how citizens vote. As the LDP became more responsive to citizens' demands for welfare and environmental measures and the opposition at the national level continued to be disorganized,

---

1. We use the terms mobilization, vote request, or vote solicitation interchangeably to refer to the process whereby citizens are asked to vote for a particular candidate. Following Rosenstone and Hansen's study of political behavior in the United States, we refer to the process whereby candidates, parties or activists personally contact people to encourage them to vote for a specific candidate as "direct mobilization." We use "indirect mobilization" to refer to the process by which leaders contact people through mutual associates, a process that can occur in networks, either informal social networks or by membership in more formal networks (Rosenstone and Hansen 1993, 26).

2. See, for example, Ward (1951); Flanagan (1968); Curtis (1971; 1988).

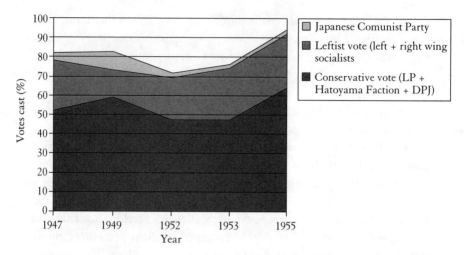

Figure 3.3. Vote choice in early postwar elections (percent of total votes cast for the respective parties). Election Department, Local Administration Bureau, Ministry of Internal Affairs and Communications.

people once again began voting for the LDP in increased numbers. They did so for the next ten years, after which support once again plummeted.

Embourgeoisement

Early research on political change among modern electorates—particularly in European countries—focused on economic factors (see Dalton, Beck, and Flanagan 1984, 15–16). The basic argument was that growing affluence produces an overlap in the income and lifestyles of the middle and working classes, contributing to declines in, or impeding the growth of, class voting.

During Japan's economic growth, blue-collar workers, many of whom had recently moved to the cities, assumed the lifestyles of the middle class and identified with the middle class on public opinion survey questions. This was strengthened by a national ideology that stressed that Japan was a homogeneous society of hardworking middle-class subjects, a rhetorical claim that was popularized in 1970s notions of a "mass education society" (Kariya 1995) and a "new middle mass" (Murakami 1984),[3] despite the

---

3. These notions aside, identification with the middle class became the norm—despite, rather than because of—objective measures of class. While the Gini coefficient was comparatively low in Japan, other measures show that in terms of class mobility,

fact that many worked in industrial jobs that were low paid and offered poor working conditions.

In the 1950s, ideological differences in Japan centered on the place of Japan in the international system (the strength of the U.S.-Japan Security Treaty, the role of the Japan Self-Defense Forces, and relations with communist nations) and the type of system that citizens sought (such as the creation of a welfare state, the role of the emperor, and, later, the power of business versus the consumer or environmentalist). The values cleavage that pitted conservatives against leftists reached its climax with the renewal of the U.S.-Japan Security Treaty in 1960, as we described in chapter 2, when supporters of the treaty and those in opposition physically battled in the Diet and on the streets.

Increasing affluence contributed to the demise of the sharply bifurcated, ideology-driven party system, by undermining the appeal of radical politics for most citizens. Living standards rose to unimaginable heights: real GDP per capita in constant prices (Laspeyres index) rocketed from $2,392 in 1950 to $24,660 in 2004 (Heston, Summers, and Aten 2006). The incredible rise in living standards occurred under LDP administrations and linked the party to the rising affluence in the minds of voters.

This affluence offset to some extent the negative impact that the demographic shifts might have had on LDP support. Added to this, and augmenting the party's support base, were: (1) the strength of the party's grassroots organization that had effectively mobilized the party's support; (2) its strength among the self-employed owners and managers of small and large businesses; (3) malapportionment; and (4) the lack of alternatives to the LDP, since during the time of the 1955 system, the opposition was radical and fragmented.

Organization of Support

Big business and small business provided the LDP with an organizational support base. At the grassroots level in the towns and cities, professional associations such as the Japan Dental Association, Japan Medical Association, and various merchants associations mobilize support for the LDP.

---

openness, and the universalistic allocation of socioeconomic status, Japan was remarkably similar to Britain and the United States during the 1970s and 1980s, and that in the 1990s and early 2000s relative mobility has been limited (Ishida 1993; 2006).

The longer people stay in communities, the more likely they are to be mobilized by these networks.

In addition, although the rural population has shrunk, in the country-side, the Central Union of Agricultural Cooperatives (Nogyo Kyodo Kumiai, or Nokyo for short, also known as JA [Japan Agricultural Co-operatives]), has played a crucial role in joining the LDP to its rural elec-toral base. The national level of Nokyo backs the LDP, as do most local branches. Nokyo has eight million members, including 99 percent of farm households (the economic incentives of membership in Nokyo are high), making it the largest political organization in Japan.

Nokyo's influence should not be exaggerated, but it has been a formida-ble force in grassroots mobilization, and its members often mobilize—or in some cases, constitute—the *koenkai,* or support organizations, of local Diet members. Nokyo also offers the candidates it supports campaign organization and staff and political funds. This is illegal because Nokyo receives state subsidies, but members manage to circumvent the law (Bul-lock 1997). Robert Bullock describes the few rural districts that are, or have been, JSP bastions and claims that between one-quarter and one-third of farmers vote for parties other than the LDP, chiefly the JSP. Farmers de-fected in huge numbers in the 1989 election to protest the beef-citrus lib-eralization agreement signed with the United States in 1988 (see Miyake 1992). Although farmers have lost some of their influence over policy, and their numbers and hence electoral clout has declined, they (and the fish-ing industry) continued to vote overwhelmingly for the LDP well into the 1990s (Kobayashi 1997, 195). As we discuss later, it was not until people in the countryside began to believe that the Koizumi reforms had negatively affected rural areas that this support abated.

Malapportionment

Unequal representation or malapportionment—the systematic variance in the size of electoral constituencies—is a feature of the Japanese sys-tem, as it is in many countries. In Japan, malapportionment gives dispro-portionate representation to rural voters, making rural votes worth more than urban votes.[4] The advantage this has given the LDP over the years can be graphically represented, as shown in figure 3.4.

4. Malapportionment in the United States is slightly different in that the U.S. Senate is deliberately malapportioned (and has become more so since its creation),

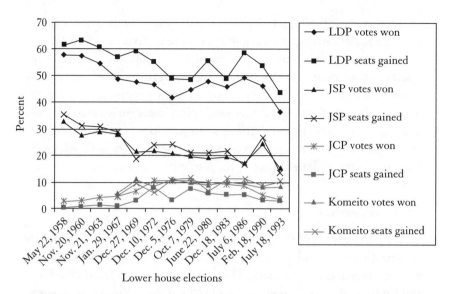

Figure 3.4. Malapportionment in lower house elections, 1958–1993. Figures are rounded, so they may not add up to 100 percent. From the 33rd election onward Okinawa-ken is included. From 1996 onward is the proportional representation portion. Figures for votes won are percentages of votes cast. Election Department, Local Administration Bureau, Ministry of Internal Affairs and Communications.

Fragmented, Disorganized Opposition and Its Support

We would expect urbanization to benefit the opposition vote, but several important factors have mitigated the potential effects of this internal migration on the leftist vote. In addition to the growing affluence of workers, unions—the "natural" constituency of the Left—were shrinking in size and the Socialists were an unattractive choice, as they were radical and increasingly out of touch with the average voter as well as lacking a grassroots organization.

The JSP periodically engaged in bitter factional in-fighting and failed to offer voters a single, clear alternative to the LDP. In 1960, for example, one of the two main labor federations, the Japanese Confederation of Labor (Zen Nihon Rodo Sodomei, or Domei for short), supported the Democratic Socialist Party (DSP or Minshushakaito), the moderately left-wing party that emerged from the split, but it could never pull in enough votes

---

granting two senators to every state regardless of population size. This results in two senators representing over 33 million Californians and two senators representing fewer than half a million citizens of Wyoming.

to threaten the JSP. Similarly, in 1978, the party split again, but the defectors, the Social Democratic League (Shaminren) never developed into a significant party (see figure 2.1). Some of the socialist factions were ambivalent about parliamentary politics and modernizing. Left-wing party activists, who cared passionately about ideological issues, influenced the party's policy platform. Long after ideological issues such as security, defense, and the constitution declined in importance for citizens, the Socialist and Communist parties continued to focus on these issues, losing potential support that a change of focus might have brought.

The Labor Movement

Scott C. Flanagan (1984) traces the Socialists' ideological rigidity to their organizational dependence on the labor movement. The JSP was never well organized at the grassroots level; instead, it depended on the General Council of Trade Unions of Japan (Nihon Rodo Kumiai Sohyogikai, or Sohyo for short), for "votes, campaign organizations and workers, funds, and even candidates" (Flanagan 1984), so when labor radicalized in the 1950s, so did the JSP. The Kishi government of 1957–60 openly proclaimed that it would seek a showdown with the JSP and the unions. The administration weakened the unions by defeating them in dramatic confrontations and sidestepped them by negotiating with "second unions." The JSP's natural constituency of union members decreased: after a huge jump in rates of unionization in the immediate postwar period, the estimated unionization rate declined from 34.3 percent in 1975 to 19.5 percent in 2003, based on Ministry of Health, Labor and Welfare data (RIALS 2007).

The JSP never really recovered from its 1969 drubbing. Its image and policies seemed increasingly out of sync with the changing world, and citizens rejected the party. The JSP continued to push for peace and focus on opposing Anpo, while the LDP had withdrawn from the debate and had adopted a low posture internationally. Citizens gradually ceased to be interested in the issue (Reed 2003), and, particularly after the oil shocks, people's concerns turned to social and livelihood issues (Kobayashi 1997, 198). The JSP's vote share declined from the 1960s onward, from 33 percent in the 1958 election to 17 percent in 1986.[5] The party did experience

5. This is the JSP vote only. The broader socialist vote includes the Democratic Socialist Party, which was at its highest in 1960 at 6% and declined thereafter.

a surge in 1989 and 1990. In 1989, led by Doi Takako (the first woman ever to head a major party in Japan), who had pushed to modernize the party, the JSP focused its campaign on corruption (after a series of LDP scandals) and opposition to the new consumption tax and defeated the LDP in the House of Councillors election. The party also did well in the 1990 general election for the House of Representatives, capturing 24 percent of votes cast, but it did not do well enough to unseat the LDP (see figure 3.4). The party was unable to build on this victory, and its support collapsed completely during the early 1990s when many of its Diet members joined other parties, particularly the DPJ. By the 2005 lower house election, the Socialist Party, renamed the Social Democratic Party of Japan in 1996, could only muster 5.5 percent of the votes cast (see figure 3.3).

Even though the JSP has been derided as a "half party" that was never able to really challenge the LDP's dominance, the JSP was not entirely marginalized. The party sometimes set the agenda for national discussion and legislation and at times was able to force concessions through procedural delays. The dramatic, sometimes violent, tactics the opposition used in the 1950s and 1960s—the fistfights in the Diet, the sit-downs in Diet corridors, the deliberate traffic jams, and the boycotts—mostly gave way to the "cow walk" (*ushi aruki*), a filibuster or delaying tactic, that they used to great effect to halt parliamentary business. Each Socialist member would rise slowly to vote and shuffle toward the ballot box using tiny steps. It could take hours for every member to vote. The Socialists showed their disapproval or tried to gain concessions by using this cow walk, or even threatening it.

It was extremely difficult for the JSP to provide a credible alternative policy platform. The socioeconomic system as a whole facilitated growth and shaped development in an egalitarian direction, thus undercutting policies around which the opposition might have organized support. In addition, the LDP was also prepared to co-opt policies that the opposition did develop and popularize when it was absolutely necessary to do so. As discussed earlier, when citizen activism surged—for example, in demands for better public services and environmental protection during the late 1960s and early 1970s—the LDP acted on these issues for fear of being electorally punished. This undercut any policy agenda that the opposition might have developed—beyond criticism of political corruption—and allowed the LDP to maintain its dominant position, which it did partly by being responsive to this new range of demands.

As we discussed, Ethan Scheiner (2005) argues that the centralized, clientelistic nature of the state has contributed to the opposition's failure in

Japan from the 1950s onward. Local-level politicians need connections to the national government to secure subsidies, thus local-level politicians who have connections to LDP Diet members do well in local elections. Failure at the local level has contributed to national-level failure by the opposition, by depriving opposition parties of candidates with previous experience. Scheiner points out that the numerous rural districts are the most prone to these practices.

Furthermore, as we discussed in chapter 2, the electoral system makes it so that candidates from the same party were running against each other, thus encouraging electoral competition among candidates based on personality and constituency services and blunting the overall importance of policy issues and political party platforms.

Fragmented Opposition: Other Parties

Other smaller parties include Komeito (the party officially became known as New Komeito in 1998), a party that Soka Gakkai formed in 1964 from its precursor, the Komei Political League.[6] Komeito is the only religious party in contemporary Japanese politics and has organized itself into a formidable mobilizing machine. Although Soka Gakkai and Komeito have been formally separate since 1970, they still maintain close ties. Analysts estimate that around half of the Komeito votes come from affiliates of the Soka Gakkai (Watanuki 1991). The party was originally radical: its policy goals included pacifism (to be achieved partially through global disarmament), humanitarian socialism (together with Buddhist democracy), and the purification of politics (Hrebenar 2000, chap. 6). Komeito also opposed amending the constitution, supported an independent foreign policy, and—most famously—committed itself to expanding welfare programs. Komeito followed an ad hoc approach in its policy stance that seemed to be aimed toward gaining popularity, and over time has become much less radical than in its early days. In the mid-1990s, Komeito merged into the New Frontier Party and when that party collapsed in 1998, reformed itself as New Komeito. From 1993 to 2009, Komeito joined various coalition governments, first in the coalition that excluded the LDP in 1993 and then as a junior partner in various LDP-led

---

6. Soka Gakkai is the largest of the Buddhist evangelical "new religions" and is the lay organization of the *Nichiren Shoshu* Buddhist Sect.

coalition governments. Support for welfare remained a steadfast policy goal throughout this period and Komeito had some significant successes in welfare policymaking.

Komeito wins around 13 percent of votes cast in lower house elections (see figure 3.4). Its support base is unlikely to grow much since it has been hurt by the dramatic slowdown in Soka Gakkai's rate of growth (Hrebenar 2000, 174), but the party is highly effective in mobilizing and organizing its support base at the polls. In the future, it could become a crucial player if neither the LDP nor the DPJ is able to form a government alone, by switching its allegiance to the DPJ.

The Japanese Communist Party's vote share in national elections reached a peak in 1972 and then declined through the 1990s, with the exception of 1996, when JCP support surged to 12 percent. In contrast, during the 1980s and 1990s, at the local level, the number of JCP prefectural and municipal assembly members rose (Berton 2000). And during the late 1960s and 1970s citizens chose JCP mayors and governors, and the party achieved even more success when it backed progressive candidates of other parties rather than running its own candidates (Berton 2000).

Other niche parties have formed, but they have ultimately failed to expand their support base beyond their core constituency (Reed 2003, 8). The LDP, too, has a history of splintering, but each time it looked as if the splintering would be a serious threat, the party managed to cling together. A prime example of this behavior was the New Liberal Club in 1976.

A group of disaffected LDP Diet members broke away to form the NLC, and as voter support for the NLC surged, it seemed as if the NLC might be able to threaten LDP dominance. Ultimately, though, the party joined the LDP in coalition, and then re-joined the LDP. The SNTV electoral system increased the difficulties small parties faced in gaining a foothold. Furthermore, the LDP's control of the budget meant that non-LDP politicians were not able to bring home pork to their constituencies the way LDP politicians could. Some analysts suggest that that control of the budget was a powerful force in keeping the LDP together.

The System Disintegrates

The structural premises that had supported the LDP system began to crumble during the 1970s and 1980s. As government spending increased, it became untenable to continue relying on deficit spending. As we mentioned in the last chapter, a proposal to introduce a consumption (sales) tax contributed to a resounding defeat for the LDP in the 1979 lower house election. During the 1980s, some administrations called for fiscal responsibility without increased taxation and pushed a small-government agenda built on a program of administrative reform.

Although the premises on which the LDP system was built were crumbling, the rural districts' disproportionate representation in the Diet, together with the clout of senior politicians from these areas, to some extent protected the system from reform. And so the system continued to function, distributing pork to the rural prefectures, which mobilized votes for their LDP representatives and kept the LDP in power. The incumbent advantage that exists in many countries was magnified in Japan by the redistributive base of LDP power, and the longevity of the party allowed it to keep delivering to its constituencies. However, many citizens, particularly those in the cities, viewed pork barrel spending as inefficient and were incensed by this apparently wasteful spending as the economy continued to flounder during the Heisei recession. Thus, reform of the LDP system itself finally emerged as a genuine political issue during the 1990s.

The Rise and Fall of the New Parties

Things looked bleak for the LDP: despite public opposition, the administration of Prime Minister Takeshita Noboru enacted the new consumption tax of 3 percent in 1989. This unpopular tax was flanked by the massive and highly publicized Recruit scandal and Sagawa scandal, which increased public anger and distrust of politics.[7] Both Prime Minister Kaifu Toshiki—after the Recruit scandal—and Prime Minister Miyazawa Kiichi (1991–93)—after the Sagawa scandal—publically promised reform, but neither delivered due to disagreement within the LDP, further angering the public.

When the LDP administration of Prime Minister Miyazawa failed to aggressively pursue reform, Hata Tsutomu, a leading reform advocate,

---

7. The Recruit scandal was an insider-trading scandal that involved some of Japan's politicians and bureaucrats receiving gifts of stock in Recruit Cosmos, a new subsidiary of the human resources company, Recruit, in return for eased regulatory supervision of the latter (Kabashima 1992). Dozens of politicians allegedly accepted bribes from the Sagawa Kyubin trucking firm; Kanemaru Shin was convicted and fined for doing so.

forced the 1993 election by having his faction (the largest in the LDP) support a motion of no confidence against the Miyazawa cabinet. Frustrated and angry (and no doubt fearful of their electoral prospects) at the lack of reform, thirty-nine members of the LDP voted against their own government in this motion (eighteen more abstained by being absent from the vote).

It looked as if the party system was collapsing as politicians broke from the existing parties to form new ones. On June 21, 1993, a group of reformers led by the LDP legislator Takemura Masayoshi, an ex-bureaucrat and former governor of Shiga Prefecture, formed the New Party Sakigake (Shinto Sakigake). Two days later, another group of incumbent LDP legislators, including the Hata faction, broke away from the LDP to form the Japan Renewal Party (Shinseito). The party was officially led by Hata, but Ozawa Ichiro, a former power broker within the LDP with an ambiguous attitude toward reform, also wielded substantial power.[8] These parties added to the new party movement that had begun in May 1992 when former LDP member and governor of Kumamoto Prefecture, Hosokawa Morihiro, formed the Japan New Party (Nihon Shinto). In December 1994, Ozawa engineered a merger of several of these parties into the New Frontier Party (Shinshinto), which only managed to last for three years before it split apart, leaving Ozawa as the leader of the much smaller Liberal Party (LP). Curtis (1999) gives a detailed description of the maneuverings and machinations of political leaders during this period. See, as well, figure 2.1 and chapter 7 of this book for an overview of the various parties.

Voters punished the LDP, and it lost control first of the upper house, in 1989, and then of the lower house, in 1993. The LDP had never seemed as doomed as it did in the wake of the 1993 general election. The party lost its majority in the House of Representatives, winning only 223 out of 511 seats, marking an end to its thirty-eight-year single-party rule. The Socialists won just 70 seats, an all-time low, while the new parties made a dramatic debut, winning a combined 103 seats. The new parties represented "change" to the electorate, and the single most powerful predictor of a vote for one of the new parties was the desire for a change of government (Kabashima 1994; Reed 1996).

The new parties "won" the 1993 election both in the sense that they enjoyed the biggest gains in seats and in the sense that they were able to deny the LDP any chance of retaining its majority by the combination of

---

8. See Otake (1997) on the formation of the new parties in the early 1990s.

seat losses and defections. The biggest loser, however, was not the LDP but the Japan Socialist Party.

The JSP was unable to capitalize on the 1989 and 1990 gains, and by 1993 they no longer symbolized change. The party had lost the mantle of being the alternative to the LDP to the new parties. The party's vote share returned to its pre-1990 pattern of decline.

In some ways, the 1993 election fits with longer-term trends. Steven Reed describes it as "a 'normal' scandal election, similar to the previous scandal elections of 1976, 1983 and 1990" (Reed 2003), that is, in the immediate aftermath of scandals, voters turn against the LDP (see figure 3.4). The difference, as Reed points out, was that in 1993 there were non-Socialist opposition parties from which the dissatisfied voter could choose.

Seizing the important opportunity to finally unseat the LDP after so many years overrode other considerations, and all the opposition forces, except the Communist Party, cobbled together a coalition government led by Prime Minister Hosokawa Morihiro (1993–94) of the Japan New Party. Hosokawa was from an aristocratic background, and although the *kazoku* (peerage system) was abolished by the Occupation authorities, he succeeded his father as the titular Daimyo (lord) of Kumamoto and titular 6th Marquis Hosokawa (he is the eldest son of Morisada, 5th Marquis Hosokawa, titular Daimyo of Kumamoto and the grandson of former Japanese Prime Minister Konoe Fumimaro). Despite his aristocratic background, he was the first Japanese leader to publicly acknowledge that World War II was a mistaken war of aggression, and he expressed responsibility and condolences to the war victims and survivors.

Increasing public distrust of politicians and dissatisfaction with politics led to a growing consensus among pundits, citizens, and some politicians that the 1955 system needed major reforms. At the time, politicians feared opposing reform and incurring the wrath of the public, especially since critics thought that the old electoral system contributed to the money-based aspect of politics and the lack of focus on party platforms (see Otake 1998).

After much wrangling, the Hosokawa government, with LDP support, enacted campaign finance reform and electoral reform. The Political Party Subsidy Law (1994) reformed the complex laws from the 1950s and established a system of state subsidies based on a party's vote share and parliamentary membership. Parties receive around $300 million per annum, supposedly not to aid individual politicians. Nevertheless, major loopholes still exist that allow Diet members who become the chairs of their local district branches to receive these funds (see Curtis 1999, 165–66). Similar loopholes exist in the regulations on corporate donations: corporations may contribute only to parties and not individuals, but little prevents parties from then passing along the contributions to individual politicians. Electoral reform created a "side-by-side" electoral system in which voters cast one single nontransferable vote in their single-member district for a candidate (there are 300 SMD seats in the House of Representatives) and one proportional representation (PR) vote for a party in one of eleven regional blocs (there are currently 180 PR seats in the House of Representatives). The system also provides unsuccessful candidates with a much-criticized "second chance": candidates who fail to be elected in their SMD race can win through inclusion on their party's PR list. These are the so-called zombie, or resurrected, winners, who rise from the dead after losing the election (see appendix A). Curtis describes why this system was adopted (1999, chap. 4).

Proponents of electoral reform argued that in the SMD portion of the system candidates would no longer compete against members of their own party, and since the districts are so large, they could no longer rely completely on a personal vote. The even larger size of the PR blocs would necessitate an electoral base beyond the *koenkai*. In addition, voters could opt to vote for a party, which again may focus voters' attention on party and national rather than local-level politics.

Reformers had all sorts of hopes for the new system, some realizable, others not. As Steven R. Reed and Michael F. Thies put it, some voters and pundits, unsurprisingly, expected too much: "They expect that all of the ills associated with the old system will be washed away with the introduction of the new one" (Reed and Thies 2001, 381). We expect that the changes will become more pronounced as voters and candidates become used to the system. Candidates cannot rely on their standard operating procedures alone, but will move toward "good election campaigning," defined by election reform architects as a party-centered, issue-oriented campaign strategy, which by extension may foster responsiveness in the resultant administration, because the party commits itself to the positions it takes during the campaign period (Dabney 2008).[9]

At the same time, however, the system imposes an alternative set of imperatives on candidates that encourages them to maintain the old ways

---

9. In contrast, McKean and Scheiner (2000) argue that the technicalities of the system will transform the PR representatives into locally based politicians who will rely on the personal vote, rather than on party or policy-based politics.

of connecting with voters. As Krauss and Pekkanen (2008) point out, most candidates are dual-listed, and two-fifths of all PR representatives are zombie winners. This large number of legislators need to focus on their constituencies, rather than on platforms or their parties. Margaret A. McKean and Ethan Scheiner argue that the dual-listing provision and the large number of zombie winners will make PR candidates into "SMD candidates-in-waiting," who are oriented to their constituents in the districts (McKean and Scheiner 2000, 447). The findings of Pekkanen, Nyblade, and Krauss (2006) support this, showing also that zombie representatives are given more than their share of party, committee, and legislative posts to facilitate their winning in their SMD constituency the next time around.

Reformers who hoped that the incentives of a new electoral system would quickly influence the behavior of parties and leaders and produce an alternation in power at the national level were unrealistic. Most scholars were more circumspect, expecting change to come about slowly. Few theories in political science are as well known and controversial as Duverger's "law" that asserts that plurality or simple-majority single-ballot electoral systems depress the number of parties and that proportional representation encourages multiparty systems (Duverger 1959). The basic idea behind the proposition is that a majority system discourages smaller parties from forming, since their potential leaders and supporters know that the system disadvantages parties that cannot win more votes than any rival in at least some constituencies, and thus discourages voters (and potential leaders) from supporting small parties for fear of "wasting" their vote. The crucial point is that electoral systems affect which parties form, run in elections, and how voters choose which party to support. As analysts are quick to point out, Duverger himself did not describe his assertion as a law, but rather as a set of pressures that a particular system exerts. Reformers hoped that with two viable parties to choose from, alternation in power would occur, but in a side-by-side system, parties and voters have to contend with the incentives of both systems.

The changes that have occurred are exactly those that Duverger would have predicted—in each election after reform, at the district level competition has moved toward two viable candidates (see Reed 2008). The existence of a single-member district system should discourage new parties from forming, since their chances of winning SMDs would be slim, and it would encourage parties to hold together to maximize their seat share, which is more or less what has happened. Consequently, at the district level, a two-party system was in place by 2003.

Once reform passed and the coalition's honeymoon period of popularity ended, public support waned, despite the initial high approval rating for the cabinet. Prime Minister Hosokawa resigned in April 1994 after only 260 days in office, after critics accused him of accepting a questionable loan during the early 1980s. The accusations were particularly damning since Hosokawa came to office pledging to clean up politics. The coalition parties appointed a new prime minister, Hata Tsutomu of the Shinseito, or Japan Renewal Party. Hata, the son of a politician (his own son would later follow in his footsteps and become a politician), had risen to be a top lieutenant in the Tanaka/Takeshita faction in the 1980s. The Hata cabinet lasted for only two months. The Social Democratic Party of Japan (SDPJ), the largest party in the coalition, defected, leaving the coalition government without a majority in parliament. Rather than face a vote of no confidence, Hata chose to resign in June.[10]

The big shock was what followed: on June 30, 1994, the Socialists joined the LDP, their historic enemy, and Sakigake to form a new coalition government. This coalition was in many ways hard to believe, since competition between the LDP and the Socialists had defined the Japanese party system since 1955. Socialist Party leader Murayama Tomiichi was appointed as prime minister and was later replaced by Hashimoto Ryutaro of the LDP.

At that time, former prime minister Takeshita Noboru reportedly claimed, "We have swallowed the Socialists and we have them in our stomach. All that remains is for the gastric juices to digest them," suggesting that they could easily restore LDP hegemony after the brief interregnum of the Hosokawa administration between August 1993 and April 1994 (Stockwin 1996). Antireform LDP politicians believed that the hopes for reform invested in the Hosokawa coalition government would founder with the return of the LDP to power (in a coalition with the JSP).

The first Socialist prime minister for almost half a century, Murayama Tomiichi, publicly apologized for Japanese atrocities during the war. He had much to contend with, both in modernizing his party and in the events that occurred during his short tenure. He tried to move his party

10. After the Shinseito merged into the Shinshinto (New Frontier Party) in 1996, Hata lost a leadership election to Ozawa Ichiro. He then formed the splinter Sun Party, which merged with the Good Governance Party (Minseito) in January 1998, which in turn merged with the Democratic Party of Japan in April 1998. Reed describes in some detail the various new parties, mergers, and splits—both proposed and actual—between 1993 and 1996 (Reed 2003, 25–61).

toward the center, much to the consternation of his radical colleagues and supporters, when he proclaimed that the U.S.-Japan Security Treaty was constitutional. His government was criticized for dealing slowly and poorly with the Kobe earthquake of January 17, 1995. The Aum Shinrikyo cult's sarin gas attack on the Tokyo subway occurred during his tenure.

Remarkably, given the confusing political maneuverings during this time, the Japanese public *was* able to make sense of it all by adjusting their attitudes to the new reality, according to data from a nationwide panel survey, the Japan Election Survey II (see appendix C). Although very few individual voters were able to follow all the twists and turns during this chaotic period, the aggregate impressions of the electorate mapped the political space with amazing accuracy. At the individual level, this process involved revising attitudes toward traditional enemies and toward their own party. Citizens accurately revised their perceptions of the political space, even incorporating the most bizarre and subtle twists of elite maneuvering (Kabashima 2004).

In Japan, as elsewhere, even though most individual voters may not be able to pass either a civics test or a quiz on current events, the electorate in the aggregate reacts in sensible ways to political events (see Popkin 1991; Page and Shapiro 1992). Though much work remains to be done explaining individual attitude change, these results tend to support the idea of a group basis for political reasoning (Brady and Sniderman 1985). People need not be particularly sophisticated to have a fairly good idea of who are friends with whom at any given time. Indeed, we may need to reconceptualize the idea of political sophistication: voters may be much more capable of keeping track of complex interrelationships among political actors than they are of understanding ideological debates among elites, policy debates among experts, or lectures on politics by academics.

Findings support the idea that attitudes toward political parties and political figures are endogenous to the political process (Gerber and Jackson 1993). Voters update their evaluations of political actors based on cues from trusted sources of political information (Lodge, Steenbergen, and Brau 1995). Though individual-level change is complex, the resulting aggregate attitude configurations tend to move in congruence with the actual political situation. Thus, for example, Socialist supporters tended to have a higher opinion of the LDP, and LDP supporters tended to have a higher opinion of the Socialists after the coalition was formed than they had before. In general, the parties within the coalitions of strange bedfellows were reevaluated to make the coalitions seem less strange.

Despite all expectations, the "new-party boom"—as the surge in popularity of the new parties was labeled—was short lived. Once the Hosokawa cabinet failed after such a short tenure, the parties lost the momentum to remain small and independent, and they were absorbed sooner or later by other parties.

As we discuss in more detail in chapter 7, the Democratic Party of Japan, formed in 1996 and then relaunched in 1998, emerged as the major opposition party. Although the party was a union of politicians from across the ideological spectrum and at the time of its formation lacked a coherent party platform, the merger was successful enough against the background of Japan's continuing recession to convince people of the DPJ's ability to become an alternative to the LDP and to vote for it in the upper house election of 1998.[11] The growing significance of a strong opposition party finally enabled these individual voters to "punish" the LDP. The phenomenon of "split voting" was notable; voters were more likely to cast their ballot for the LDP candidate in their constituency than they were to pick the LDP in the PR vote. In addition, the rise of unaffiliated voters as an important electoral group contributed to the LDP's losses in 1998, although it held on to its ruling-party status.

Hashimoto resigned following the LDP's disastrous showing in the 1998 upper house election and was replaced, after a primarylike selection process, by Obuchi Keizo, the least popular of the candidates with the public, in what Reed describes as "a triumph of 'politics as usual'" (Reed 2003). Obuchi, a second-generation politician who inherited his father's constituency in Gunma Prefecture when he was twenty-six years old (and whose daughter took over the seat when he died) was bland and self-effacing; the foreign press considered him so unappealing that they nicknamed him "cold pizza." Despite his self-deprecation, he was a skilled LDP insider, a master at Nagata-cho (Japan's Capitol Hill) games, having earlier seized control of the Takeshita faction from under the noses of top lieutenants and presumed heirs Hashimoto Ryutaro, Hata Tsutomu, and Ozawa Ichiro. The public warmed to him, but he served up more of the old LDP extremely expensive economic stimulus packages, including giving away 35 million shopping vouchers, all of which proved ineffective in jump-starting the economy. Gregory Noble stresses that, despite

11. Of the 126 seats at stake in the July 1998 election, the LDP captured just 45. Since it held only 58 of the seats not up for election, it was left with a total of 103, far short of a majority.

his lack of charisma, Obuchi was actually highly effective at shepherding proposals through the legislative process, including the details of ministerial organization and various regulatory reform measures originally proposed by Hashimoto (Noble 2005, 18). The Obuchi administration abolished the long-standing practice of senior bureaucrats, rather than cabinet ministers, answering questions in the Diet and also introduced Question Time, during which the prime minister is grilled by the opposition (see chapter 6).

To gain a majority in the lower house, the LDP had formed a coalition with the Liberal Party (known as the JiJi coalition to combine the first character of each party's name) in January 1999 and then included the reformed Komeito in October (JiJiKo). The Liberal Party left the coalition in April 2000, and Prime Minister Mori Yoshiro (2000–01) turned to the New Conservative Party (a party that had split from the LP) as a coalition partner. The three-party coalition made up of the LDP, New Komeito, and the New Conservative Party won a clear majority in the 2000 lower house election, but it was a galling victory: the coalition lost 64 seats, whereas the DPJ gained an additional 35 seats. These trends were more pronounced in the PR portion than in the SMDs. Yet victory gave the LDP the confidence to ignore the reality of its position.

Dealignment in Recent Elections

Upper House

Voters' preferences are clear in the House of Councillors elections from 1983 through 2007. The LDP was defeated in 1989 because of a backlash against the consumption tax and because of the spate of scandals. In the 2001 election, on the other hand, the LDP cruised to a resounding victory based on voters' hopes for—and approval of—the newly formed Koizumi administration (table 3.1).

The LDP's PR vote in the upper house election, since it regained control of the House of Councillors in 1994, peaked in 2001; then it fell in 2004, and again in 2007, when the LDP lost control of the upper house. To some extent these changes have been affected by structural factors, particularly the shift from binding to nonbinding lists of candidates, but they are still clear indications of voters' preferences. The only time the LDP did really well was in 2001, when Koizumi was enjoying an approval rating of nearly 80 percent. The LDP performed better under Koizumi than it did before, but 2001 still left an impression of an LDP defeat because commentators

TABLE 3.1
LDP Upper House Election Results, 1983–2007

	1983	1986	1989	1992	1995	1998	2001	2004	2007
Prefectural districts[a]	49	50	21	49	31	30	44	34	23
Proportional representatives[b]	19	22	15	19	15	14	20	15	14
Total seats won	68	72	36	68	46	44	64	49	37
Percentage of seats gained	54	57	29	54	37	35	53	40	45

Note: Figures do not include candidates who joined the LDP after an election.
[a]1983–1998: 76 seats (77 in 1992, including one by-election seat); 2001: 73 seats.
[b]1983–1998: 50 PR seats; 2001: 48 seats.

overestimated the "Koizumi effect." These results are closer to reflecting the "true" strength of the LDP, although they are still generally well above the 1998 levels.

The LDP did poorly in the 2004 upper house election, but the Koizumi effect—even in its reduced form—saved the LDP from total disaster, since Koizumi was still able to pull in urban votes, making him indispensable to the LDP. In contrast, the DPJ's vote share and the number of seats the party gained were remarkable. The DPJ was probably helped by being able to present a consolidated slate of opposition candidates. In addition, the party gained from the peculiarities of the upper house electoral system, which resulted in the number of seats being disproportionate to the number of votes gained.

In the run-up to the 2007 election, various events over which it had no control worked in the DPJ's favor. The Social Insurance Agency had lost track of 50 million public pension payment records; people feared for their pensions and doubted the competence of the government. DPJ politicians, particularly Nagatsuma Akira, the intense former journalist, won much media coverage for savaging the LDP over the lost pension records. Public anger and frustration boiled over on this issue, and support for the Abe cabinet plummeted. Shortly thereafter, the press reported on a string of financial and other scandals involving members of the cabinet, further depressing the level of support. *Kakusa*—economic disparities— became a buzzword, touted in the media and by classic LDP politicians as the downside of LDP-enacted neoliberal reform (discussed further in chapter 6). The LDP was thrashed in the July 29, 2007, upper house election, winning only 37 of the 121 seats up for election. This was the party's worst trouncing in an upper house election since 1989 when it won only 36 seats. Komeito won just 9 seats. In contrast, the DPJ won 60 seats, making it the largest party in the upper house. At first glance, a huge change in voting preferences seems to have taken place between the upper house elections of 2001 and 2007. However, if we exclude the Koizumi elections, the 2007 election was actually just a normal election in which the LDP did not do that well. As we discuss in more detail later, commentators blamed reinstating the postal rebels and the pension fund fiasco for the LDP's loss. The Kabashima Research Group–Shimbun Public Opinion Survey showed that social security and taxes were top concerns for voters, which taken together was the Achilles' heel of the LDP.

Lower House

A look at recent lower house election results shows that in the November 2003 election the Koizumi effect was substantial in the PR districts, but that it was less so in SMDs. Although, overall, the DPJ was no match for the LDP, the LDP's hold on power was not that solid. It barely managed to stay even with the DPJ in the PR segment, largely thanks to the Koizumi effect; it could not have won as many single-seat races as it did without Komeito's help; and the DPJ proved to be a formidable opponent in many other races. On the other hand, Kabashima and Sugawara (2004) conclude that the DPJ's success in the PR portion of the vote in 2003 was mainly thanks to its merger with the Liberal Party. The DPJ made substantial inroads in the single-member intermediate districts that had been dominated by the LDP, and it solidified its foothold—albeit a small one—in rural districts.[12] At that point, the DPJ could not topple the LDP, as long as the LDP remained in coalition with Komeito. The DPJ, meanwhile, could hold its own in the PR districts, but it was no match for the LDP-Komeito alliance in many SMDs.

The dependence of LDP candidates on the votes and support of Komeito supporters and members of Soka Gakkai, the lay organization of the Nichirin Buddhist sect that backs Komeito, is a further important feature of recent elections (see Kabashima 2000; Kabashima and Sugawara 2004). Analyses of lower house elections suggest that the LDP is increasingly reliant on Komeito's vote-mobilizing machine and that by 2003 the LDP would have lost nearly half of its SMD seats without Komeito's well-organized mobilizing machinery (Kabashima and Sugawara 2004).[13]

12. Even with 21 additional seats, the DPJ only secured 105 seats, just over a third of the 300 being contested.

13. The LDP's reliance on Komeito increased despite Koizumi's popularity. This was partly due to the DPJ's merger with the Liberal Party, which enabled it to mount

After the 2000 election, some Komeito members complained that they got little back from this arrangement, so the party asked the LDP to reciprocate in 2003 by encouraging its backers to vote for Komeito in the PR portion of the vote. This presumably contributed to Komeito's PR vote share increasing by almost one million in 2003—a vote gain that translated into two additional seats. (See Kabashima and Sugawara [2004] for a more detailed analysis of the LDP's reciprocation.)

Explaining Voters' Choices

We analyzed the influences on citizens' vote choice in three elections, using data from public opinion surveys that were conducted after each election.[14] We chose the 1986 election, a pre–electoral reform election, to compare with the postreform elections in 1996 and 2003.[15]

We investigated whether the same subgroups of people who voted for the LDP in 1986 still did. Has electoral reform made a difference? Is mobilization still as important as some analysts assert? Have the ways in which politicians try to reach voters changed? (See this chapter's appendix 3.1 for a table detailing the variables that we included.)

Our results clearly demonstrate the changing relationship over time between voters and parties, but they also show that some factors continue to influence voting preferences. (See this chapter's appendix 3.2 for these results.) To interpret the results more easily, we concerted them to the probability that a hypothetical median voter would vote for each party (see King, Tomz, and Wittenberg 2000).[16] In 1986 the median voter was a female, white-collar worker, educated to high school level (middle school in the prewar system), and forty-eight years old. She had lived in a town with

---

a more effective challenge to LDP candidates in single-seat races and to actually defeat many of them.

14. We use data from the Akarui Senkyo Suishin Kyokai (Society for the Promotion of Clean Elections House of Representatives) election surveys. The ASSK is a cross-sectional survey that is conducted after each election. The respondents are drawn from a stratified nationally representative sample, and the interviews are conducted face to face. See appendix B for details.

15. We estimated a multinomial logistic regression model for each election.

16. It is difficult to interpret the coefficients directly, inasmuch as the model is nonlinear and the effect of estimated coefficients depends on the values taken by the other coefficients. We do not convert all coefficients to probabilities since we are more interested in broad over-time patterns.

TABLE 3.2
The Declining Probability of the Median Voter Choosing the LDP

	Probability of Voting for the LDP	Probability of Voting for the Left or DJP
1986	.72	.18
1996	.74	.05
2003	.42	.37

Source: Calculated from the analyses presented in chapter appendix 3.1. Data are from ASSK data sets.

a population greater than one hundred thousand for more than twenty years and was a member of one or more community groups. Of the policy issues, she only considered taxation when making her vote choice. By 1996 the median voter was fifty-three, but otherwise she had the same profile as her counterpart twenty years earlier. By 2003 the only difference was that she considered the economy and pensions when deciding how to vote.

The results show a stunning drop in support for the LDP: in 1986 a median voter's probability of voting for the LDP was .72, whereas the probability of a vote for the Left was a meager .18. By 2003 the probability of a median voter choosing the LDP had dropped to .42, and the probability of a vote for the DPJ was .37 (see table 3.2).

What influenced this transformation in vote choice? First, confirming previous research, we found that citizens' policy preferences did not usually influence their vote choice, after taking into account other causes of the vote. On the very few issues that were important, the DPJ was unable to make a mark. Concern over welfare stands out: Before 2003 citizens who were concerned about welfare were less likely than were others to vote for the LDP. But by 2003, this had reversed;[17] since the LDP are in coalition with Komeito, and Komeito has been able to push through a number of pro-welfare reforms, Komeito's pro-welfare image may have rubbed off on the LDP. At that point in time, the DPJ had failed to associate itself with welfare policy in ways that the old leftist parties used to. Similarly, the DPJ was unable to capitalize on the issue of defense. People who thought defense was important were less likely to vote for the LDP in 1986 and 1996, but by 2003, this had ceased to matter and it did not sway voters toward any party. These findings confirm the decline of the old Anpo cleavage-related issues: the salience of defense for mainstream

17. This relationship is also evident in cross-tabulations.

conservative voters has faded, but for a small minority of left-wing voters, minimizing security ties with the United States continued to be important at least until 1996.

Surprisingly, for a party that has been linked with agricultural interests and support for farmers, agricultural issues only benefited the LPD in 1986. This may be because farmers turned against the LDP because of declining protection, or it may be a statistical artifact—very few respondents claimed that the issue was important.

The indirect measures of social integration—length of residence and size of the community—were both generally influential: urban voters and the geographically mobile tend to be anti-LDP. However, membership in community networks is not associated with voting for the LDP, with the exception of *koenkai* membership, which confirms the strength of the LDP's grassroots organization.

Membership in trade unions was important in 1986, but since then it has not been significant. Similarly, members of professional associations do not always vote for the LDP. Rather than a union leader or merchants' association leader delivering a bloc of votes to a specific candidate, economic interests may influence the voting preferences of members of occupation-based networks. Union members and members of professional associations have a common understanding of what is good for them as individuals and their group, but this is only one element in the calculus of vote choice.

Thus, mobilization in networks is not as important to voting preferences as some analysts claim. Other research, too, confirms this (see Richardson 1991). The U.S. literature on participation provides a theoretical framework that can be used to understand why participation in Japanese networks does not predict vote choice. James Q. Wilson (1973) argues that a variety of incentives explain people's participation in organizations. These may include material incentives, specific or solidary incentives, or purposive incentives. Material incentives are tangible rewards for participation that can be priced, such as a job, tax reduction, improvement in property values, or personal services and gifts for which one would otherwise have to pay, and so forth. Solidary incentives are less concrete than material rewards and include offices, honors, and deference. Such solidary incentives develop from the social interaction that comes with participation, but they must be enjoyed by the group as a whole. These benefits include the fun and friendliness of participating in groups, and the sense of exclusiveness and esteem that the group as a whole enjoys. Solidary incentives "depend for their value on how the recipient appears in the eyes of others ...[they] depend on the maintenance of valued social

relationships" (Wilson 1973, 40). Purposive benefits are the intrinsic rewards that come from the sense of satisfaction of having contributed to
something worthwhile (Wilson 1973, 30–51).[18]

In Japan, too, a unique mix of these incentives spurs individuals to participate in community groups. Solidary benefits are particularly important: many people join neighborhood and community groups as a duty to
enjoy the benefits associated with membership such as deference, friend-
ship, and solidarity.

People often join community groups because they feel pressure to do
so, and they often participate even though they do not want to. For them,
the fulfillment of obligation and a sense of duty to maintain cordial social relations outweighs the costs of membership. In the case where participation is reluctant and feelings of group solidarity are low, it would be
surprising if voting decisions were highly correlated with group membership. Furthermore, the percentage of citizens who actually report being
mobilized through these groups is extremely small, so it seems as if their
influence has been exaggerated. It is unlikely that the community groups
that support the LDP are geographically concentrated such that their impact is not discernible in a national sample. There is little doubt that community groups are stronger in rural areas and in small- to medium-sized
cities (see, for example Richardson 1991, 337). For the effects to wash out
like this, though, suggests that the pro-LDP groups are not as widespread
and influential as commentators assume.

Older people are more likely than younger people to vote for the LDP.
Analysts often assume that voters with low educational attainment are
more likely than their highly educated counterparts to vote for the LDP.
The implicit assumption seems to be that that voters with less education
lack political knowledge and have a greater sense of deference, and that
deference and ignorance translate into votes for the LDP. Yet this is not
the case. Educational attainment does not influence the probability that a
citizen will vote for the LDP.

18. There are important differences. In Japan, for example, members of ostensibly nonpolitical groups report vote solicitation through their membership in various
community and occupation-based groups. In the United States, Jan Leighley has found
that although unintentional mobilization occurs in nonpolitical and political groups,
intentional mobilization is restricted to political groups (Leighley 1996). There is a
greater degree of crossover between these two types of mobilization in Japan, partly
due to the sponsorship of nonpolitical groups by politicians and the endorsement of
politicians by nonpolitical groups.

In sum, up until the 1980s, the LDP had a solid block of support that it could take for granted, but this is not the case in the first decade of the 2000s. Politicians—from the LDP and the DPJ—cannot rely on community or occupational networks to pull in votes, but need to vary their standard operating procedures. Parties thus turn to their policy platforms, stressing their differences from other parties and their respective manifestos. Most policy preferences do not typically influence a person's vote, but, at the same time, citizens do claim to be interested in policy issues. The electorate is capable of a number of splits along policy lines, so politicians have to decide which of the potential splits—if any—will be more effective and advantageous to them as vote-garnering strategies, and they will have to determine how to package their policy platforms to attract support. But, as we discuss in chapter 4, basing a campaign on a manifesto is not without difficulties. The convergence between party leaders proposing a line of division and the audience/electorate responding is an unpredictable process that involves trial and error (see Manin 1997).

Unaffiliated Voters

Finally, we turn to the increasingly important and growing segment of independent voters. Researchers at the University of Michigan developed the concept of party identification, or "the sense of personal attachment which the individual feels toward the [party] of his choice" (Campbell, Gurin, and Miller 1954) four decades ago as a part of their model of vote choice that emphasizes the social-psychological aspects of party identification; that is, people learn to identify with a political party through a gradual process of socialization (Campbell et al. 1960); and while party identification is not immutable, it is fairly stable (Niemi and Weisberg 1993).

Party identification is also crucial in explaining Japanese voting behavior, and the declining rates of citizens who identify with any party suggests that rather than supporting the LDP as the only party capable of governing, there are increasing numbers of "critical citizens," as Pippa Norris (1999) and others describe them.[19] When LDP support is high, the number of independents declines, that is, the evaluative component of party identification is important and is based in part on citizen assessment of

---

19. Using the Michigan model outside of the American context is not without controversy. See Richard Johnston (1992) for an argument criticizing the portability of the concept of party identification.

policy performance and conduct in office (Pharr 2000). Whereas analysts used to consider independents as having less formal education and less interest in politics than their counterparts with party attachment, since the 1970s, this had changed, and the number of educated independents has increased. These independents are people who fail to see the relevance of party politics to their everyday lives and who are cynical about politics and less satisfied with the governing party than those with party attachments (Miyake 1991, 226–60).

Data from aggregate studies show that the number of independents is slowly increasing, although aggregates probably exaggerate the overall stability by canceling out actual change at the individual level. Independents increased from 24 percent of the population in the early 1970s to 30 percent in 2003 (figure 3.5).

Support for the LDP fell throughout the 1990s recession. Even though this was not reflected in a "vote the rascals out" mentality, fewer people identified with the party. Voters did not enact a simple reward-punishment scenario during the recession, probably because responsibility for the economy in Japan is not clear, and, as Pharr points out, for a country that has become wealthy so recently, the economic circumstances are comparatively good (Pharr 2000).

Analysis of panel studies shows greater instability than does analysis of aggregate patterns (Kabashima et al. 2000).[20] Research shows that party support has become much more fluid with the collapse of the LDP's monopoly during the mid-1990s (Kabashima and Ishio 1998). Kabashima Ikuo and Ishio Yoshito (1998) examined the instability of party identification among eligible Japanese voters during the 1993–96 period using data from a panel survey. Because the party system was highly unstable at that time, it is unsurprising that only about a quarter of the sample consistently identified with the same parties. A majority of voters were either inconsistent partisans (24%) or occasional partisans (48%) during the survey period; they changed the parties they identified with or became nonpartisans at least once. Membership in religious organizations had a stabilizing effect on party identification, as did—in general—favorable opinions about preexisting parties, whereas people who were critical of contemporary politics and the politically apathetic had a weaker sense of party identification. These people may be attempting to induce political

20. Other studies claim 30–40% of the electorate do not identify with any party (Flanagan and McDonald 1979, cited in Flanagan 1984).

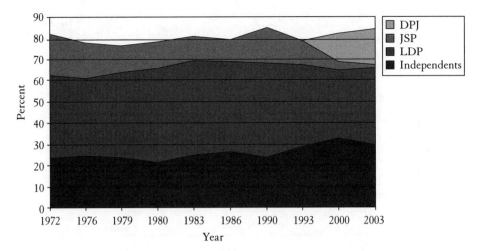

Figure 3.5. Party identification. ASSK, various years.

change by changing their party identification, and their party identification may be conditional on the performance of the political parties.

Koizumi understood that without the support of the nonaligned, predominantly urban voters, the LDP could not survive. But the urban floating voters did not continue to support the LDP after Koizumi; they were largely "one-issue voters," and for them, postal privatization was symbolic of their broader desire for reform. They turned from the LDP, partly because the apparent ramifications of structural reform were unpopular (although urban voters still objected to perceived wastefulness), but also because the LDP returned to being the party it had been before Koizumi and no longer symbolized change.

In focusing on reforming the system that urban voters objected to, Koizumi transformed LDP support. No party can hope to retain control of the government over the long term without building support in urban areas. Most voters live in urban areas, and the electoral reforms of 1994 went some way toward rectifying the overrepresentation of the rural districts; but until Koizumi, the LDP was unable to win over urban voters.

The LDP's share of the PR vote in the 2000 and 2005 elections is graphically represented according to electoral districts' level of urbanization (figure 3.6). Trends are clear: In 2000, although the LDP did poorly, the DPJ failed to win a majority, but the split between the big cities and the less-urbanized regions was crystal clear. In the big cities the DPJ came out ahead, while in the rural areas the LDP won by a landslide. Urban voters were not enamored with the LDP under Mori Yoshiro. By 2005, however,

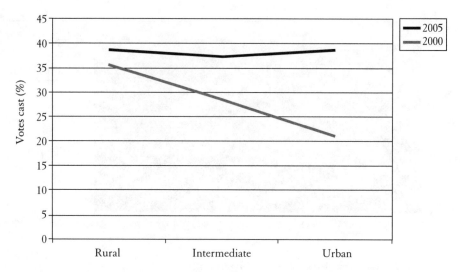

Figure 3.6. Koizumi seizes the urban vote, 2000–2005. Kabashima and Sugawara (2005).

a sea change had occurred: people in urban districts were almost equally as likely as rural voters to choose the LDP, largely due to independents voting for the LDP. This urban support, in direct contrast to the classic rural strength of the LDP, was key to the success of Koizumi's LDP. Under Koizumi, politics was no longer driven by the contest between the interests of rural voters and those of urban voters. (We discuss this period in more detail in the following chapters.)

Japanese voters were persuaded by Koizumi's call for reform—especially urban voters—and supported him, causing a blip in the LDP's overall declining vote share. The pinnacle of his electoral success was the 2005 general election. Even at its height, however, Koizumi only managed to capture a small percentage of the swing vote (see figure 3.4), But because of distortions in the way seats are allocated, this produced a huge number of seats.

Given this transformation, the LDP's return to the old system—which relied on the support of rural voters—has not pulled in similar levels of support. In the 2007 upper house election, the LDP lost the support of independents in the provinces and in the metropolitan areas where it had won big in 2005 (see Kabashima and Imai 2008). By 2005 Koizumi had successfully, albeit temporarily, altered the structure of the LDP's support base. He understood that it was no longer enough, and increasingly economically unfeasible, to rely on rural voters and distribute benefits to them. Instead, it was crucial to win support from a broader base that encompassed independents and urban voters (groups that were growing, while the LDP's traditional support base was shrinking). Winning support from a broader base was essential since the organizational and institutional support base that had helped the LDP maintain its long dominance was crumbling, a story we return to in our discussion of the 2009 election in chapter 7.

Appendix 3.1

Influences on Voting

	1986		1996		2003	
	LDP	Left	LDP	Left	LDP	Other
Issue Considered						
Welfare	−0.602*	−0.322	−0.570*	−0.725*	0.281**	0.282**
	[0.148]	[0.192]	[0.209]	[0.197]	[0.127]	[0.138]
Environment	0.163	0.022	−0.026	−0.056	−0.079	−0.171
	[0.269]	[0.330]	[0.278]	[0.261]	[0.185]	[0.203]
Prices 1986, 1996	0.085	0.332	0.406**	0.09	−0.05	−0.406*
(Economy 2003)	[0.153]	[0.198]	[0.204]	[0.191]	[0.125]	[0.136]
Education	0.359	0.275	0.553	0.438	0.185	0.297
	[0.193]	[0.238]	[0.306]	[0.290]	[0.180]	[0.187]
Ethics	−0.5	−0.097	−0.869*	−0.355	n.a.	n.a.
	[0.280]	[0.333]	[0.275]	[0.245]		
Agriculture	0.918*	0.365	0.5	−0.289	0.219	0.049
	[0.262]	[0.375]	[0.375]	[0.372]	[0.313]	[0.359]
Taxation	−0.263	−0.124	−0.27	−0.1	0.062	0.133
	[0.152]	[0.198]	[0.205]	[0.193]	[0.133]	[0.144]
Defense	−1.242*	−0.778*	−1.113*	−0.53	−0.197	−0.147
	[0.229]	[0.288]	[0.428]	[0.369]	[0.169]	[0.182]
Constitution	0.151	−0.225	−0.415	−0.516	−0.301	0.206
	[0.344]	[0.423]	[0.476]	[0.428]	[0.217]	[0.218]
Reform 1986, 1996	0.051	−0.027	0.114	0.056	−0.12	−0.122
(Fiscal reform 2003)	[0.201]	[0.255]	[0.228]	[0.214]	[0.153]	[0.166]
Pension	n.a.	n.a.	n.a.	n.a.	−0.23	−0.243
					[0.138]	[0.149]
Socioeconomic variables						
Cohort	0.154**	−0.082	0.255*	−0.1	0.164*	0.029
	[0.064]	[0.081]	[0.083]	[0.076]	[0.048]	[0.051]
Education	0.038	−0.273	−0.054	−0.14	−0.106	−0.128
	[0.124]	[0.160]	[0.113]	[0.106]	[0.067]	[0.074]
Gender	−0.181	−0.492**	0.302	0.451**	0.135	0.218
	[0.158]	[0.204]	[0.209]	[0.197]	[0.127]	[0.139]
White-collar	0.287	0.102	0.276	−0.166	0.02	−0.02
	[0.152]	[0.195]	[0.217]	[0.205]	[0.131]	[0.141]
Integration						
City size	0.101	−0.304*	0.291*	0.017	−0.120**	−0.089
	[0.065]	[0.084]	[0.085]	[0.079]	[0.051]	[0.055]
Duration	0.123	−0.231**	0.270**	0.075	0.128	−0.146
	[0.084]	[0.100]	[0.116]	[0.102]	[0.079]	[0.077]

APPENDIX 3.1—cont.

	1986		1996		2003	
	LDP	Left	LDP	Left	LDP	Other
Network membership						
Trade union	−1.609*	−0.767*	−0.441	−0.076	−0.454	−0.468
	[0.216]	[0.258]	[0.318]	[0.282]	[0.309]	[0.332]
Religious	−0.448	1.971*	0.231	0.172		
	[0.398]	[0.368]	[0.567]	[0.541]		
Community	−0.184	−0.346	−0.101	0.055	0.056	−0.119
	[0.178]	[0.223]	[0.228]	[0.213]	[0.122]	[0.133]
Koenkai	1.052*	0.716*	1.046*	0.762**	0.740*	0.397
	[0.207]	[0.256]	[0.328]	[0.321]	[0.198]	[0.228]
Professional	0.077	−0.547	0.107	−0.214	0.739*	−0.145
	[0.241]	[0.373]	[0.356]	[0.354]	[0.248]	[0.324]
Constant	0.162	2.790*	−1.544**	2.797*	−0.557	0.929**
	[0.584]	[0.716]	[0.707]	[0.632]	[0.445]	[0.457]
Observations	1567		2063		1736	

Source: ASSK.

Cells are multinomial logit coefficients with standard errors in brackets.

The dependent variable is the respondent's reported vote in MMDs (1986) or SMDs (1996 and 2003). This is a three-category variable: the LDP, leftist parties (the JSP and the Japan Communist Party), or other. In 1986 we combined the NLC with the LDP; in 2003 we combined the CP with the LDP. The comparison groups are other parties in 1986 and 1996 and the DPJ in 2003.

We have noted changes in questions used.

Missing coefficients were either not included on the survey or excluded from the analysis.

* significant at 1%; ** significant at 5%

Appendix 3.2: Factors Influencing Voting Preferences

We included the following variables in the analysis to gauge the influence of the consideration of policy issues on vote choice: agriculture, prices (1986 and 1996), pensions (2003), welfare, taxation, education, defense, the environment, the constitution, reform (fiscal reform 2003), ethics, and economics (2003) (1 if considered, 0 otherwise). As control variables, we included (1) measures of network integration: membership in a community network, professional association, trade union, or *koenkai*, or a religious alignment (1 if member, 0 otherwise); (2) social integration: length of residence (4-category variable) and community size (5-category variable); and (3) sociodemographics: age (6-category variable in 1986 and 1993; 8-category variable in 2003); education (elementary, middle, upper; 3-category variable in 1988; 4-category variable in 1996; 5-category variable in 2003); gender (1 if female, 0 otherwise); and white-collar status (1 if white-collar, 0 otherwise).

4

Changing Media, Changing Politics

The media have become crucial mediators in the relationship between citizens and politicians. Researchers used to pay little attention to the media, assuming that media effects were minimal and that local-level personal ties dominated citizens' political decision making. But social change and accompanying changes in media output have contributed to a shift in relations between politicians and the public.

Television news and how news stations report on politics have changed beyond all recognition since the 1980s. Television stations now broadcast more about politics, not only on hard-news shows, but on soft-news shows, "infotainment" shows, and even on variety shows. The public has responded enthusiastically to these programs and, hence, researchers are now increasingly paying attention to the media.

We begin this chapter by describing how television has changed and then outline previous research on the media, focusing mainly on television and newspapers. Next, we discuss why voters increasingly use the media as a source of political information and how adroit politicians and leaders can—and increasingly must—exploit this. As a case study, we examine how Koizumi Junichiro was able to exploit the changes in both television and print news to become leader of the LDP, although his successors were not able to exploit these changes. The media did help Fukuda Yasuo's (2007–08) selection as prime minister by emphasizing how popular he was in the party. But as prime ministers, none of Koizumi's immediate successors—Abe Shinzo, Fukuda Yasuo, or Aso Taro—were media performers in the same way that Koizumi was. In addition, they did not need to use public support as leverage to push through reforms, since they were not far from the LDP mainstream, but they did need public support to stay in office. We look at the DPJ's media strategy in chapter 7.

Changing Media

Television stations have transformed the style and content of their news programs, increasing the number of softer news programs that they broadcast. The national public broadcasting corporation Nippon Hoso Kyokai (NHK) once dominated television political reporting, providing news that was "dry, scrupulously non-interpretive, and visually staid" (Krauss 2000; 2002, 7). *News Station* (TV Asahi 1985–2004) pioneered a radical change in 1985. Anchored by Kume Hiroshi, a former quiz and pop music show host, *News Station* quickly became the most popular news program (see Taniguchi 2004). This program broke with news conventions; in contrast to the NHK anchors, Kume did not simply review events, he analyzed the news and often added sarcastic or humorous comments.

Other stations introduced their own more relaxed-style news programs to compete with *News Station*. The "wide shows" (the largely daytime soft-news programs) then countered by increasing their political coverage, adding interpretation and analysis of political events in an entertaining, accessible way.

Soft news is now broadcast virtually all day, every day, and since relatively few households have cable television, viewers mostly watch broadcast television. Wide shows vary in how entertainment oriented they are, from *Sunday Project*, a more serious weekend talk show (that began as a wide show hosted by a comedian, but hardened up), to softer shows like *Mino Monta no Asa Zuba* (Blunt Mino Monta's Morning Show). Many air during the weekday daytime and target housewives and the elderly. Politicians regularly appear as guests on wide shows and on the evening variety shows—they are now staples on shows such as *Beat Takeshi no TV Tackle* (Taniguchi 2007).[1]

Increases in political news in the last couple of decades are due both to mainstream news programs adopting wide show techniques and also

---

1. Only 40% of households have cable TV (Ministry of Internal Affairs and Communications 2007, cited in Taniguchi 2007).

to wide shows increasingly reporting on politics. Simultaneously, and probably not coincidentally, more people find television useful in deciding how to vote (Krauss and Nyblade 2004). Citizens have come to expect politicians, particularly party leaders, to appear on television, and politicians do so because they expect to accrue electoral benefit from appearing on television (see Taniguchi 2004). That is, politicians realize that they cannot rely on their personal vote, but need to reach out to the public via the media.

This is particularly the case for DPJ politicians. The general perception is that political news overwhelmingly covers the government and that coverage of the DPJ in opposition is rare. Whereas some LDP members feel that the media is a bothersome, non-LDP politicians are dissatisfied with their limited media coverage, a perception that influenced the DPJ's strategy to win media approval (see Osaka 2007), as we discuss in chapter 7.

Research on Politics and the Media

Until the mid-1990s, very little research existed on media effects in Japan.[2] Some commentators expressed concern about the media being the "fourth estate" (*daiyon no kenryoku,* or "fourth authority"), but with a few notable exceptions (Feldman 2002; Hoshi and Osaka 2006; Pharr and Krauss 1996) most scholars considered the importance of the mass media in Japanese politics to be negligible. But as the mass media changed and politicians changed the ways they responded to the media, research on media effects exploded, and many researchers now argue that the media have influenced the style and content of politics (Hoshi and Osaka 2006; Ikeda 2004; Osaka 2006; Takenaka 2003, 206–18; Taniguchi 2004; Yamada 2004).

Among scholars who have focused primarily on the media, one of the big debates is whether or not the media are neutral. Some argue that the institutionalized system of reporting fosters dependence by reporters on official sources and that it promotes self-censorship. Critics frequently

2. George DeVos states: "The interaction between mass media and protest movements and subsequent political or legal responses is a topic that needs further consideration." Ellis Krauss adds, "One weak point...in...almost every...study of protest in post-war Japan [is] the lack of attention to the role of the mass media....The media are the crucial 'silent partner'...transmit[ting] the facts that a 'problem' exists....Much more could be done" (DeVos 1984, 4, 172).

argue that the system of press or reporters' clubs, in which reporters are assigned to specific "beats" that allow them to develop close, institutionalized relationships with their sources, contribute to bias in their reportage. Uesugi Takashi (2006), a former freelance journalist who is now deeply critical of his own and other journalists' coverage of Koizumi, argues that the traditional relationship between politicians and reporters in which reporters competed with one another for access to party leaders meant that reporters were often too close to their sources, relied too heavily on their briefings, and were not used to investigating matters on their own. Karel van Wolferen strongly argues that newspapers uniformly disseminate prostate information (Wolferen 1989, 93–100).

Some of the criticisms underestimate the changes that have occurred in television news programming, ideological differences among the newspapers, and the critical faculties of journalists. Ellis Krauss, for example, argues that until the mid-1980s newspapers were *not* consistently supportive of the state, much less so, in fact, than was television (Krauss 1996). Furthermore, television news programs now include a plethora of hard- and soft-news programs, the hosts of some of which offer a critical perspective. Critics also ignore the different ideologies of the newspapers and the existence of a substantial number of newspapers that are not part of the press club system.[3]

A few studies do present the media as a force for change: as early as the 1970s, most elites in Japan believed that the media were the most influential group according to Kabashima and Broadbent's 1986 survey. Although this survey documents elites' perceptions of group influence, rather than influence itself, many other studies demonstrate that the media publicize nonmainstream social movements, and in doing so have contributed to change.[4]

Various authors in the Pharr and Krauss anthology *Media and Politics in Japan* (1996) demonstrate that the media have both supported and

---

3. Content analysis confirms what is blindingly obvious to laypeople: of the large circulation dailies, the *Asahi* was the most critical of the government, followed by the *Mainichi*, the *Yomiuri*, the *Nihon Keizai*, and the *Sankei*. The latter two were usually supportive of the government (see Feldman 1993, 28–29). In addition, sports newspapers are tabloid-style mass-circulation papers that constitute approximately 10% of all newspapers (NSK 2008) and are not part of the institutionalized system of politician-journalist relationships.

4. See, for example, Kabashima and Broadbent (1986); Groth (1996); and Reich (1984). Other prominent cases include the agitation by some television journalists for a non-LDP government in 1993.

criticized the state, that is, they combine the roles of government watchdog and government lapdog. Pharr describes this synthesis of criticism
and support as a "trickster" role (Pharr 1996, 35).[5] Laurie Anne Freeman,
on the other hand, argues that the watchdog, servant, or spectator meta-
phors do not fully describe the media. Instead, they are "coconspirators"
with the state, benefiting from close ties with official news sources (Freeman 2000, 21).

Krauss argues that the media's criticism of the state helped maintain
LDP dominance: criticism ensured that the LDP responded to changing
public opinion, as expressed through the media, even if the response was
sometimes belated (1996, 360). The media legitimized LDP dominance,
because they gave prominence to subordinate social and political groups,
informing and mobilizing public opinion within the established conservative framework. The government was then forced to respond to the
demands of the public for fear of being punished electorally, and the resulting policy output then contributed to public satisfaction. As we discuss
later, the media were explicit in stating that the public were dissatisfied
with the LDP and that the LDP needed to listen to the rank and file (and
to select Koizumi).

Media Effects

Although older research suggests that the media in Japan can only influence young people and certain limited subgroups in portrayals of unique
events,[6] the media are crucial in transmitting information to the public. In
focusing on some people and events, rather than others, the media *set the
agenda,* affecting which issues and people citizens believe are salient. Further, the media *prime* the public by focusing on some aspects of national
life while ignoring others, thus setting the terms under which political

5. This ambiguity is reflected in the attitudes of some journalists: On the one hand,
journalists believe that they should confront the regime, and see journalism as affecting the functioning of government (see Kim 1981). On the other hand, newspapers are
ostensibly committed to the policy of *fuhen futo, churitsu koisei* (impartiality, political
neutrality, and fairness) (Feldman 1993, 16–18).

6. Flanagan (1996, 279) notes two such studies. The first implies that the media
politicize young university students (Akuto et al. 1978). The second suggests that
media portrayals of the Lockheed scandal had a substantial effect on the vote choice
of citizens with high media exposure who considered corruption a problem, had no
party identification, and were highly educated (Flanagan 1991).

judgments and choices are made (Iyengar and Kinder 1987, 4).[7] And, as we discussed above, more recent research suggests that media effects are much more pervasive than previously believed (Hoshi and Osaka 2006; Taniguchi 2007).

Taniguchi Masaki (2007) provides evidence of substantial media effects. Using findings from experiments, he argues that politicians gain votes from appearing on wide shows, but only if they can combine policy content with entertainment.

Hoshi Hiroshi and Osaka Iwao (2006) claim that the wide shows were responsible for Koizumi's popularity. They also point out that producers of wide shows consider the economic value of stories in their decision making (Hoshi and Osaka 2006). Producers chose to cover Koizumi because he would be popular with viewers. Newspapers and commercial television stations are businesses, and as such they are motivated by economic concerns. As James T. Hamilton (2004) demonstrates in his analysis of U.S. news, news content is a commodity, driven by the interests of viewers and readers, and the value of those consumers to advertisers. Product differentiation means that the news content depends not only on the audience, but also on what other news outlets are producing. Uesugi (2006) provides a further concrete example of this. He argues that the media censored themselves and were overly concerned with reader opinion with regard to Tanaka Makiko. The self-confident populist daughter of former prime minister Tanaka Kakuei, and herself foreign minister under Koizumi, became very popular with the media and the public by being outspoken and critical of the LDP and by exposing corrupt practices within her ministry. Because she was so popular at the time, the media did not report extensively on various controversies in which she was involved, since full disclosure would have made her look bad.[8] The media did not simply provide news about people and events that citizens did not directly experience, but as businesses, they were aware of, and selected news on the basis of the points of view of their audience. Because the media did not discuss Tanaka's behavior at length, her popularity was not threatened, but when Koizumi eventually did fire her,

---

7. Zaller (1992) refers to the resulting issue statements as "top of the head" responses.

8. These included various diplomatic blunders, leaked ministry information, a missing ring (that she accused a bureaucrat of stealing), a missed visit to the imperial garden, and an argument in the Diet with top bureaucrat Vice Foreign Minister Nogami Yoshiji in which they contradicted each other.

his popularity plummeted. (We discuss the ramifications of this incident in the chapter 5.)[9]

How Koizumi Stole the Leadership of the LDP:
The Backstory

By 2000 public opinion had turned against the Liberal Democrats. The Obuchi Keizo administration enacted a series of controversial bills, including legislation implementing the new Guidelines for Japan-U.S. Defense Cooperation, bills formally designating the national flag and national anthem, and a measure authorizing wiretapping in investigations of organized crime. These were all ideologically sensitive pieces of legislation, and many voters thought they should have been handled cautiously, with more convincing arguments advanced in their support. In addition, the Obuchi administration's staggeringly expensive spending on public works and other purposes looked like indiscriminate largesse, particularly to many urban voters. As the months passed, the administration's rate of support fell (see Kabashima 2000).

When Prime Minister Obuchi suffered a stroke on April 2, 2000, and later died, Mori Yoshiro, the LDP secretary-general at that time, replaced him. The LDP had viewed Mori as a caretaker when he took office in April. Commentators expected Obuchi's sudden incapacitation and death to produce a sympathy vote for the party, but any chance of this happening was squandered by Mori's repeated blunders, and soon his popularity—and that of his party—plummeted. Mori was the foil to Obuchi's bland self-effacement. Mori was always something of a preposterous figure, a beefy former rugby player from a family of well-off farmers. His father and grandfather had both been mayor of their town. He spent two years as a newspaper reporter and six years learning the ways of Nagata-cho as an aide to politicians before being elected to the House of Representatives for the first time in 1969 (see Kawachi 2000). He was an integral part of the money politics system that voters had turned against; he had been tainted by the Recruit scandal and had been trade and industry minister and then construction minister in the 1990s. In addition, his frequent lapses in judgment were widely reported in the media. He was dogged by persistent but unconfirmed press reports that he was arrested while

9. Tanaka Makiko left the LDP in 2003 and in August 2009 joined the Democratic Party.

frequenting prostitutes as a college student and that he had improperly secured membership in an expensive private golf club. He was also forced to acknowledge the accuracy of press reports that said he spoke at a wedding in 1995 that was attended by members of a major crime syndicate (French 2000). He caused controversy with repeated slips of the tongue, saying, for example, that some teachers were controlled by communists and describing Japan as a divine nation ("*kami no kuni*") with the emperor at its core. Critics jumped on this comment as echoing Japan's militaristic past, particularly in conjunction with his use of the loaded prewar term "*kokutai*" (national polity). He tried to explain this comment, but his failure to retract it made the situation even worse (Masuzoe 2000). He became described invariably as "the gaffe-prone Mori," and critics talked of him having "the heart of a flea and the brain of a shark." His poor judgment depleted the public's patience even further; after hearing that a U.S. submarine had accidentally hit and sunk the Japanese fishing boat *Ehime Maru* during an emergency surface drill on February 9, 2001, killing some students and teachers, he continued with his round of golf.

By February 2, 2001, only 14 percent of the electorate expressed support for the Mori cabinet (*Mainichi Daily News* 2001). LDP party members were bracing for defeat in the upcoming July 2001 House of Councillors election.

It was time—yet again—for the LDP to sink or swim.

In the normal scheme of things, Koizumi would not have become leader of the LDP. Usually, either the head of the biggest faction within the LDP becomes the leader or faction leaders get together to decide on a party leader in the infamous smoky backroom deals. Koizumi lacked an organized Diet support base within his own party and he was not even a member, let alone a head, of a faction. LDP members nicknamed him *henjin,* or "the freak," for his policy preferences, antipathy toward his own party, and his forceful personality. The cartoon in figure 4.1 shows Koizumi's slim chances of becoming leader just a couple of years earlier. Besides his lack of popularity in the party, he lacked the ministerial experience that the LDP usually considered necessary. Koizumi had run unsuccessfully for the presidency of the LDP twice (in 1995 and 1998). Yet in 2001 he won. He did so by courting popular support through the media.

Why Did the Media Matter So Much?

The media were able to exert influence on Koizumi's selection by setting the agenda of what was important; this was heightened because the public increasingly look to the media for political information, and they do so because of long-term demographic change and systemic factors, including changes to the electoral system and changes in the way the LDP selects its leader.

Long-Term Trends

Economic growth and the concomitant increasing levels of affluence, higher levels of education, greater geographic mobility, and urbanization have transformed Japan. Images of a village postmaster successfully "gathering" votes from the whole village for the LDP do not aptly describe contemporary Japan. Even residents in the remotest village can access information from various sources. They are connected by communication and transportation networks and enjoy more open lifestyles, which drastically reduces the importance of the political recommendations of local notables. Political information from the media is readily available, newspaper subscription rates are high, and television broadcasts more political information than ever before. Flanagan suggests that the rise of the mass media has directly undermined patron-client models of politics and brought Japan closer to the democratic ideal (1996, 281). In addition, tightening budgets are likely to be a major constraint on clientelistic spending (Scheiner 2005). When traditional means of mobilizing the vote are severely constrained, politicians are forced to forge connections with voters through other means, and reaching voters through the media is one way of doing this.

Systemic Change since the 1990s

Added to these long-term fundamental changes, was the electoral system for the lower house that was introduced in January 1994, which also increased the importance of citizens' evaluations of party leaders in their vote choice.

As we discussed in chapter 3, changes to the electoral system encourage voters to focus less on individual politicians and more on parties and party leadership, although politicians do have a dual set of incentives to be more party/policy oriented and at the same time to maintain their koenkai and focus on constituency service. Elections under this system demonstrate the importance of citizens' evaluations of party leaders: voters' antipathy toward former Prime Minister Mori and subsequent warmth for Koizumi had clear effects on the ways they voted (Kabashima and Imai 2001).

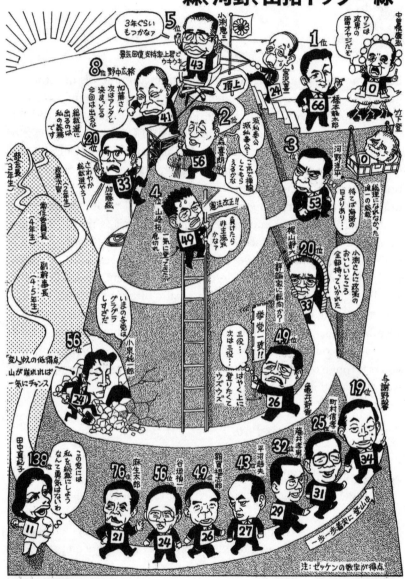

森、河野、山拓トップ一線

イラスト・松村宏

Figure 4.1. The LDP promotions derby. The politicians' rankings (the number on top of each politician) were calculated from the party and government positions held throughout the 1990s. The more important the position, the more points awarded. For example, being prime minister nets 6 points and so on down to committee member, which nets 1 point. Points appear on the politicians' bibs.

Nakasone (top right): Hey, I'm still the kingmaker!

Obuchi (5): At this rate, I could be here for three years or so.

Caption: Feeling on top of the world thanks to recovering economy and high approval ratings.

Nonaka (8): Kato-san, you'll have your chance next. Keep out of this!

Kato (20): It's my solemn duty to run in the leadership race.

Mori (2): For the greater good of the party, I'll stand down.

Thought bubble: This should smooth my way to the top.

Kono (3): Good things come to those who wait.

Caption: The one prime minister who will never be.

Kajiyama (20): Mr. Obuchi stole all of my brilliant ideas.

Caption: Second career as political commentator?

Yamasaki Hiraki (4): If I lose I'll have to find myself another faction.

Caption: Sharp rise but losing steam

Constitutional reform!!

Kamei (49): Next stop, near the top. Next stop…

Caption: Itching to take the party mantle

Koizumi (56): The LDP needs to get its act together.

"The freak" caption: So much the outsider that if the LDP falls apart he might have his chance.

Arrow caption: Up-and-coming stars

Tanaka Makiko (138): Hmmm, this party doesn't have the guts to make me prime minister.

Aso Taro, who placed 76th in 1999, actually became prime minister less than a decade after this cartoon was published.

Source: Matsumura Hiroshi, copyright 1999. Data collected by the Kabashima Seminar 1999. This cartoon was originally published in the *Asahi Shukan,* July 9, 1999.

Selection Rules

In the past, the LDP had used some variation of a backroom decision by the leadership, a Diet caucus election, or a primary to select their president. The process is often just an exercise in public relations, given that Diet members have more votes than do the prefectural chapters, and assuming that faction members vote according to the direction of faction leaders. The leader of the biggest faction is then able to select the leader, often after interfactional consultation.[10] The LDP changes the rules instrumentally since the party executives (*shikkobu*) choose which rules to follow. Both the prefectural chapters and newspaper editorials pressured the LDP to reform itself because of voter hostility. In 1998 the leaders bowed to this pressure and changed the rules so that both Diet members and party representatives from the forty-seven prefectures voted, but Diet members still had the most votes, so the faction leaders could control the process. In 2001 the prefectural chapters, responding to the public's antipathy toward Mori,[11] and anticipating a loss in the coming election, demanded and won more say in the procedure.[12]

Although Diet members still had more votes than did the prefectural chapters, Diet members knew the prefectural results when they voted. That means a Diet member's vote choice could be swayed if a candidate won the prefectures, instead of faction leaders completely controlling the process. In addition to local political activists, the primary electorate includes groups such as the Nurses Association, which pays their party membership dues, increasing the importance of being able to appeal to the general public rather than just to party activists.

Newspapers pressured the LDP to be more open and accessible. For example, the *Asahi* explicitly cautioned at the beginning of the 2001 campaign period:

> Diet members should vote in line with the primary elections. A leader who lacks popular support cannot exercise full leadership, let alone prevail in the July election....The public will be watching closely to see how the LDP picks its leader. Approval ratings for

10. Stephen Reed argues that the primaries were really just extensions of factional voting.

11. The executives who selected Mori opposed the primaries.

12. LDP members of the Diet were assigned 346 votes, and 141 votes were assigned to the prefectural chapters (3 votes per prefecture).

the LDP have already fallen below the 30 percent level. To continue the conduct of politics with the same inward-looking mindset that prevailed when the LDP ran everything alone is a recipe for self-destruction. (Asahi News Service 2001b)

Koizumi took advantage of the changes in the selection rules for the LDP president that increased the voting power of the prefectural chapters of the party. He needed to appeal directly to the rank-and-file members, since he lacked a support base in the party. To do so, Koizumi provided a dramatic story of intraparty conflict that the media would report. Almost all newspapers and news programs were eager to cover the same story in the same way. In this case, "pack journalism," in which all publishers and producers ensure that they are covering the same stories as everyone else, prevailed. The tendency toward pack journalism, or *toku ochi kyofusho* (phobia of missing out on pack-covered stories), is strong, and some researchers criticize the tendency and condemn the similarity of reportage it produces (see Feldman 1993, 28). The thematic similarity between the newspapers is tempered by their different ideological positions, so news from the different outlets is not identical. But news providers want subscribers to know they are not missing important stories, and they will continue stories with which people are familiar, which means covering the same stories as other news sources (see Popkin 2006, 330). In this case, newspapers and wide shows reported the compelling story of conflict within the LDP and the public's desire for change.

In 1995 the newspapers framed Koizumi as a sacrificial candidate, running only so that the shoo-in winner would have someone to run against. In 1998 they framed him as a neoliberal "lone wolf" trying to win over his colleagues. In 2001 Koizumi and Hashimoto Ryutaro were the two main contenders for leader. Initially, Hashimoto seemed likely to win because he was head of the party's biggest faction and had organizational clout with the rank-and-file members. Koizumi bypassed the party network and communicated directly with the public through the media. Although personalized media-oriented politics predate Koizumi, he represented a quantum leap in this long-term trend.[13] The strategies he used to become leader are dramatically different from previous political practice.

13. Previous work demonstrates that the importance of the prime minister has been increasing for two decades and over the same time citizens have become increasingly reliant on the mass media for political information (Krauss and Nyblade 2004).

To be popular among the rank and file, Koizumi needed to distance himself from his own unpopular party. After Mori, party members were dismayed by the prospect of another unpopular president leading the party to defeat in the upcoming election. The compelling story of conflict and human interest particularly appealed to the softer news (Osaka 2006; Popkin 2006). The newspapers often referred to Koizumi as the "reformer Koizumi," an advantageous label when the same newspapers implicitly considered reform a necessity, with little debate over the appropriate kind of reform. John Zaller describes such representations as "frames of reference"—news stereotypes—that the media present to the public with no alternative visions of the issues (Zaller 1992, 9). The necessity for reform became virtually a consensus issue: to be popular, politicians had to be reformists. By connecting Koizumi to these aspects of national life, the media *primed* citizens for choosing a reform-minded leader.[14] Koizumi argued for a new approach to intransigent political and economic problems that only a "reformist" could handle. The press agreed, portraying him as someone who could bridge the gap between the public and the LDP and reinvigorate its popular support.

The media also buttressed Koizumi's strategy in the ways that they chose to describe the other contenders. Hashimoto also advocated reform, but some of the newspapers continually reminded their readership of his disastrous previous tenure. Newspapers could equally—and accurately—have described Hashimoto as a former prime minister who achieved a number of significant reforms during his tenure and someone who was brave enough to lose office after introducing a necessary—but unpopular—tax. But this was not the story the media chose. Instead they framed Koizumi as the more interesting story and portrayed his proposals and eccentricities in a favorable way. Newspaper coverage of Koizumi emphasized that he "stood apart from other candidates by pressing for immediate fiscal and administrative reforms" (Maejima 2001).

In the debates between the contenders for LDP president, Koizumi's sound-bite descriptions of his proposals, such as "reliance on government spending is tantamount to addiction to drugs" earned widespread coverage in newspapers. Koizumi presented his pithy proposals as if they were the only solution to the country's woes, regardless of the pain they would cause the populace, or the LDP. Of the candidates, Koizumi was the most

---

14. We expect broad similarities between the Japanese and U.S. publics in the way elite cues are internalized.

fired up by the party's plummeting popularity and the most outspoken in calling for change in the party: his sense of crisis resonated with party members.

The media framed what should have been an open-and-shut Hashimoto victory as a newsworthy "horse race," an exciting event, with a clear frontrunner, two ideologically indistinguishable also-rans, and an outsider with ideas. The Jiji Press news service gave a strong boost to Koizumi right at the beginning of the campaign by setting an agenda that described Koizumi as a winner before there was any clear evidence that this was the case. Jiji reported the results of its survey of secretaries-general and other senior officials of the LDP's forty-seven prefectural chapters on April 12 under the headline "Koizumi in Slight Lead among LDP Local Chapters." In fact, as the report stated, only eight chapters preferred Koizumi, and six preferred Hashimoto, with a majority—twenty-eight prefectures—not responding to the survey.

Not only did the newspapers report on Koizumi in a positive light, they also reported on him slightly more often than they did on the other contenders. We use data mainly from the Asahi group; this group includes the *Asahi Shimbun*, Japan's second-largest-circulation newspaper, and two news magazines, the *Asahi Shukan* and *Aera* (most newspapers and news programs chose to discuss the race in similar terms). From the beginning of April to the day before the Diet members' vote, Koizumi averaged over ten mentions a day in the Asahi group newspapers and newsmagazines, whereas Hashimoto averaged nine. We would expect the official posts held by the other two at that time to inflate their average mentions in the news, but Kamei, chair of the LDP Policy Research Council averaged eight, and Aso, state minister for economic policy, averaged six (see figure 4.2).

Political scientist Otake Hideo argues that Koizumi is the quintessential Japanese-style populist, who shares much in common with U.S. populist leaders such as Ronald Reagan. As Otake (2003) describes it, Koizumi used television to appeal directly to people using ordinary language, in contrast with the language usually favored by politicians and bureaucrats (see Otake 2003, 110–31). In fact, there is little that was "Japanese-style" about Koizumi's populism: Koizumi's personalization of politics fits well with Kurt Weyland's (1999; 2001) definition of "populism" in Latin America and Eastern Europe (see Yamada, 2004). Weyland defines *political* populism as a strategy by which personal leaders appeal to a heterogeneous mass of followers who feel left out; leaders reach followers in a direct, quasi-personal manner that bypasses established intermediary organizations (particularly via television) and uses parties as "personal vehicles"

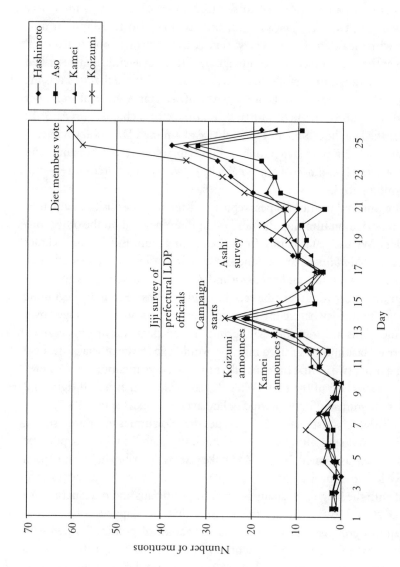

Figure 4.2. Newspaper coverage of the LDP presidential candidates, April 2001. Data compiled from the *Asahi Shimbun* Kikuzo database.

(Weyland 1999, 381–82). Furthermore, in contrast to established notions of economic populism that embrace excessive government spending, according to Weyland, political populism and neoliberalism are compatible in that they both have anti–status quo orientations: some interest groups have considerable political influence, and populist-neoliberalism condemns such groups, which include established politicians and government bureaucrats, as serving "special interests."

Koizumi ably combined populism and neoliberalism, an ideological combination that made painful measures politically viable. Despite his evident popularity, Koizumi denied that he was a populist, claiming that since the reforms that he proposed were "painful," they—and he—could not be populist. However, in truth, Koizumi's reforms stemmed from his opposition to what he perceived as big government. Inefficiency and waste became important targets for the proponents of reform, and eliminating them became important components of populism. For his rhetoric to be plausible, he needed to seem to be powerless, ordinary, and virtuous.[15] Furthermore, as Yamada Masahiro, a professor of political science at Kwansei Gakuin University points out, some sectors of the electorate may not have known the details of Koizumi's neoliberal reform policies but used their own anti–status quo sentiments as voting cues (2004, 4).

In sum, to become popular, Koizumi stressed the difference between himself and his opponents.[16] Local party members believed that "politics as usual" was discredited and no party insider could win. Koizumi earned favorable coverage at a time when the LDP's survival was threatened. He succeeded in positioning himself in the media as the solution to the LDP's declining popularity.

Koizumi, as the outside candidate, scored a landslide victory in the local primaries, coming out with about 90 percent of the electoral votes assigned to the prefectures. It was difficult for party leaders to reject the rank-and-file position, particularly in the light of the overt media pressure on the LDP to listen to prefectural demands. Despite the fact that the public could not participate, the sheer amount of media coverage of the race ensured that the race was held under public scrutiny. The newspapers, in particular, framed the election as a way for the LDP to regain the trust of the public by being open and free from factional control, putting pressure

15. Otake (2003) describes Koizumi in these terms, claiming that they are elements of Koizumi's populism.

16. Bernard Manin argues that in contemporary "audience democracies" it is crucial for leaders to do this (Manin 1997).

on Diet members not to go against the choice of the prefectures. Koizumi gained support, as Aso Taro commented after losing, "because he was the antithesis of the traditional LDP politician" (*Japan Times*, April 25, 2001). Koizumi gained momentum from taking the prefectures: Diet members, left to their own factional allegiances, might have chosen Hashimoto. But the Diet members knew the overall trend of the prefectural results, and many of them were then forced to go with the choice of the prefectures. Koizumi was formally confirmed prime minister two days after winning the presidency of the LDP on April 24, 2001.

Some commentators criticized the media coverage of Koizumi as excessive, complaining that it helped increase both his, and the LDP's, popularity. Not without justification, at the end of the LDP election, Representative Eita Yashiro, from the LDP's Public Relations Department, expressed his gratitude on national television for the media coverage of the LDP's presidential election. The public could not vote in the primaries, but the candidates were able to convey their messages to the prefectural party representatives and the Diet members from the streets during a twelve-day campaign period through the ever-present media. According to Nomura Takehiko, the candidates appeared on more than twenty talk shows (*Washington Times*, July 27, 2001). Nomura quotes Kawada Etsuko, an independent member of the lower house, as saying, "I was startled to see the massive coverage of the LDP race, in which the public couldn't participate. That coverage was an anomaly. It seems that television programs [during the LDP race in April] were created to make Mr. Koizumi a leader."

Koizumi's strategy paid off in terms of the media coverage he earned. A comparison of newspaper articles demonstrates the extent of Koizumi's media "honeymoon." A straightforward comparison of the press coverage of Koizumi with his three predecessors in the three months before and after they became prime minister shows that Koizumi fared worse than the three others until he became prime minister (see figure 4.3). But in the month of the primaries, and the three subsequent months, the aggregate volume of information in the media exceeded that of his predecessors (with the exception of the month in which lower house elections were held). We discuss the rest of Koizumi's tenure and his media-related popularity in chapter 5.

Party executives subsequently changed the rules so that Diet members would not know the prefectural results when they next voted. This meant that Diet members could vote according to factional allegiance not prefectural preferences and avoid criticism from the media, presumably

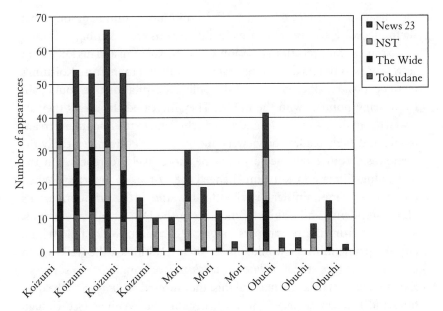

Figure 4.3. The television honeymoons of Koizumi, Mori, and Obuchi (first six months of each administration). Compiled from data collected by the Kabashima Seminar.

to prevent another Koizumi-like situation in which a candidate took advantage of the selection process, using the changes that party executives mistakenly thought would be cosmetic. Diet members who know the prefectural primary results are in a very different position than when they do not know the results. But this is only important when there is a candidate who can appeal to the prefectures and who is not the choice of faction leaders.

Koizumi's Media Strategy

Koizumi responded to the changed media as no other prime minister had done and crafted for himself a personality, in contrast to most of his predecessors: he was a character, and the public responded to the media portrayals of this new-style prime minister, who had permed hair and loved karaoke, noodles, and Elvis.

Koizumi played on the idolization that occurred during the "Koizumi boom" period. The LDP produced and sold around three million dollars worth of Koizumi dolls, masks, cell-phone straps, and posters. At the end of June, the LDP hung a gigantic poster of Koizumi on the outside of their headquarters (see figure 4.4). Koizumi himself admitted, somewhat shame-facedly, "It's really big, isn't it? But dreams are better big."

To cement his precarious position as leader, Koizumi and his long-term secretary, Isao Iijima, devised several new strategies to increase Koizumi's media exposure, since he needed the political capital that he could gain from being popular with the public. They increased the access they allowed the mainstream media and also reached out to the non–mainstream media and their readers or viewers and provided a dramatic, easily digestible story that the media would be more likely to report. On the first point, Iijima and Koizumi changed the system of reporting. When a previous prime minister returned to the *Kantei* (the prime minister's official residence and Cabinet Office) from the Diet or other functions, journalists from the newspapers, but not television, would follow him, and the prime minister would answer their questions as he walked into the residence (the so-called *burasagari shuzai,* or hanging onto sources). Koizumi and his team changed all this: they limited *burasagari* to the daytime and focused on television journalists in the evenings (see Uesugi, 2006); they broke with tradition and began allowing television cameras into the prime minister's official residence to cover Koizumi's meetings with reporters and they introduced daily press briefings in May 2001. All of this resulted in Koizumi's comments and image being broadcast directly on television.

Unusually for Japanese prime ministers, the Koizumi team also increased their exposure in the soft-news outlets: Koizumi barraged the wide show–watching public with appearances. The more relaxed format of the wide shows was an ideal stage for Koizumi, since, fairly unusually among Japanese politicians, he was a master among the "entertain-ized" politicians, barraging viewers with television appearances (Taniguchi 2004). He was able to communicate in an engaging and entertaining manner, and his humor and direct personal speaking style bridged the gap between himself and his audience (Feldman 2002).

Koizumi was also willing to bypass the official press club attached to the prime minister's office to court non–press club tabloids and soft-news magazines. He reached beyond the party faithful and appeared on chat shows. He attended televised sports ceremonies and gave interviews to sports newspapers (Ishizawa 2002; Taniguchi 2004), tabloid-style mass-circulation papers that constitute approximately 10 percent of all newspapers in Japan, according to the annual survey by Nippon Shimbun Kyokai (NSK, or The Japan Newspaper Publishers and Editors Association) (2008). Sports newspapers rarely meet with prime ministers, so the

Figure 4.4. Koizumi Junichiro. Copyright *Sankei Shimbun*.

journalists all wrote positive articles about Koizumi. Ishizawa cites this ability to increase his exposure among sports fans as one example of Koizumi's mastery of media strategy—the ability to reach beyond people who are interested in politics and who read political articles in the mainstream press (Ishizawa [2002] quoted in Taniguchi 2004).

Stringent restrictions severely limit candidates' paid access to advertising on television and in newspapers.[17] One way around these laws is for candidates and politicians to appear on chat shows, particularly the wide shows. Koizumi and his cabinet became such regular television guests that at one stage his cabinet was dubbed the "Wide Show Cabinet" (see figure 4.2).

Although some commentators denounced Koizumi's media appearance and catch phrases as the "dumbing down" of politics, his popularizing could equally be seen as a democratizing of politics. The cozy, mutually beneficial relations among bureaucrats, politicians, and political journalists were ruptured as Koizumi sought—and gained—media collaboration in taking his politics directly to the public and asking for their approval.

The first major challenge he faced was a mere three months after his selection as prime minister—the July 29 upper house election. Before Koizumi took the helm of the LDP, the LDP's electoral strength had plunged in upper house elections throughout the previous decade. They took a particularly bad pummeling in the 1989 upper house election (following the introduction of the unpopular consumption tax), to the point where they only won 45–46 seats (see chapter 3).

Japan, in common with a number of Western societies, has no socioeconomic or cultural cleavage that is more important and stable than others that politicians could draw on in selecting salient policy issues to enable them to win votes. Under these circumstances, leaders may be able to mobilize the electorate around a number of different policy issues (Manin 1997). Koizumi chose a seemingly unorthodox issue, namely, that Japan should carry out the necessary structural reforms even if this caused negative economic growth in the short run; the public would have to suffer "pain" for "gain." But at the same time, he stressed that the LDP, and the LDP's support base, would not be spared: he was widely quoted as advocating "reforms sparing no sacred cow" (*seiiki naki kozo kaikaku*). This was a stunning pledge from the leader of a party that suckled on the udders of sacred cows before riding them to market.

---

17. These restrictions lead commentators to conclude that the media in Japan have minimal impact on election campaigning (Curtis 1988, 167).

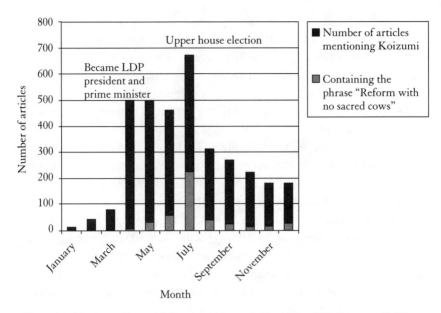

Figure 4.5. Newspapers' love of Koizumi and his sound-bite politics, 2001. Data compiled from the *Asahi Shimbun* Kikuzo database.

In 2001 alone, the Asahi group reported Koizumi's catch phrase 422 times, and selected it as one of the year's top phrases (see figure 4.5).[18] Again, this was a case of mutual manipulation: Koizumi repeatedly used the phrase in the campaign, but the newspapers chose to repeat this phrase rather than reporting on other aspects of the campaign.

Through the media, the telegenic Koizumi continued to present his policies and relationship with the LDP in sometimes astonishing, but highly popularizing, ways. Koizumi's carefully cultivated "I don't play by the rules" image allowed him to take risks to court the soft-news media and their audience, risks that previous prime ministers would not have considered. On July 8, 2001, for example, combining entertainment with easily digestible policy intent, Koizumi appeared on *Hodo 2001* (Fuji TV), where he talked about music and tore up a piece of paper that had "*teiko seiryoku*" (the forces of resistance) written on it: it was part of his stated desire to "smash the LDP."[19]

18. Kikuzo database.
19. See Taniguchi (2004) for further descriptions of Koizumi's performances on television.

Koizumi demonized as the "forces of resistance" those politicians in his own party who opposed his proposed neoliberal economic reforms and who tended to rely on distributing largesse. He attached this pejorative label to any politician who got in his way, particularly politicians from the Hashimoto faction, the largest group within the LDP and one of Koizumi's fiercest intraparty opponents. He portrayed himself as engaged in a "civil war" with the antireformists (Osaka 2006).[20]

The mass media, particularly the wide shows, consider war and conflict to be commodities that interest the viewer/consumer, as measured by ratings/sales (Osaka 2006). News programs eagerly reported on this drama, which in turn mobilized popular support for Koizumi. Crucially, Koizumi portrayed this conflict in an accessible way. He provided the media with a ready-made image—the underdog battling entrenched interests—for people who prefer a personal connection and human interest in politics.[21] As a result, Koizumi enjoyed a much more extensive television honeymoon in the first six months of his administration than did his predecessors (see figure 4.2).

Fukuda Yasuo's Selection

Following Abe's brief tenure in office, the media were instrumental in the selection of Fukuda Yasuo as LDP president. Initially, Aso Taro seemed like a shoo-in to replace Abe. Aso had come in second to Abe in the previous LDP presidential election just one year earlier; he was an experienced cabinet minister, with an outstanding political lineage, who had held various party appointments. Fukuda, on the other hand, was only in his sixth term in the House of Representatives, and his only cabinet experience was as chief cabinet secretary (albeit under two prime ministers). Although cabinet secretary is an important position as "the face" of the party, constantly in the public eye, and although Fukuda's father had been prime minister, which lent him additional recognition, by the traditional LDP selection criteria, he lacked the breadth of ministerial experience that is usually considered necessary (see Takenaka 2007).[22]

20. Although Osaka is describing the 2005 election, the same could be said of the 2001 selection process.

21. Popkin (2006) describes how U.S. news was tailored for people who prefer these kinds of personal connections.

22. Usually, having previously been foreign minister or finance minister is considered necessary. LDP criteria may have changed because the 2001 administrative

Three factors changed the expected outcome prompting Fukuda's unexpected victory: party dynamics, the media publicizing his support within the party (although it turned out that his support levels were lower than expected), and his support among the public. When Fukuda announced his candidacy, LDP factions began to line up behind him. Newspaper reports emphasized that eight of the nine factions supported Fukuda, making a vote for the more hard-line Aso seem like a lost cause. Fukuda eventually won with almost 63 percent of the total vote, far fewer votes from both the Diet members and the prefectures than his aides had predicted (Kawashima and Yoshiyama 2007). It seems plausible that if the media had described the race as close, as it actually turned out to be, Aso might have won more votes.

Fukuda's image as a consensus-based decision maker, that is, an old-school LDP decision maker, was probably crucial to his gaining the support of the factions. Koizumi's very different top-down style was still fresh in the minds—and curdling in the stomachs—of old-style politicians and swaying many party members toward Fukuda (see Takenaka 2007). In addition, Fukuda was more popular with the public than was Aso, and the media's emphasis on his popularity and factional support were important factors in his selection.

---

reforms made the position of chief cabinet secretary more important than previously. Shinoda (2006) describes the position as almost that of a deputy prime minister. The chief cabinet secretary is now empowered to mediate between ministries in disputes, and given that positions of bureau chief and above are approved by the cabinet, the chief cabinet secretary effectively gets to screen these appointments.

5

Citizens and the Prime Minister

Studies in political science often describe citizens as uninvolved in politics, seeing them as passive spectators rather than active participants in the political process (Hrebenar 2000, chap. 1). During the 1955 system, when people did engage in politics, it was in clientelistic relations at the local level, with politicians providing patronage to their districts and constituents reciprocating with their votes on election day. National-level politics and who the prime minister happened to be mattered little. Before the 1980s, for the general public, the prime minister's role and image was indistinct from support for the ruling party (Krauss and Nyblade 2004). The few academic studies of the Japanese prime minister's role describe the position as weak, constrained by informal power structures, lacking in formal resources (Krauss and Nyblade 2004, 358), and less important than the role of prime ministers in other countries. So it is hardly surprising that the general feeling in Japan was that prime ministers were fairly unimportant.

However, the resources of prime ministers and the options available to them have increased (see chapter 6), and citizen oversight of the prime minister has grown. Correspondingly, Krauss and Nyblade show that the importance of the public image of the prime minister has grown significantly in the past few decades (Krauss and Nyblade 2004).

Citizens generally have had more control over the prime minister than some accounts of politics accord them—pundits generally believe that prime ministers must resign if their approval rate falls below a certain threshold. As Masuzoe Yoichi (2000), a former assistant professor at the University of Tokyo, sometime LDP cabinet minister, and very frequent TV guest puts it, "In general, a support rate of under 30% is considered a yellow light for a Japanese prime minister, and a rate of under 20% is considered a red light."

Masuyama (2001) partly concurs and shows that the probability of a prime minister resigning depends on his approval rate among the public and on the power balance in the lower house. Even though the upper house is less powerful than the lower house, the power balance in the upper house has probably grown more important since it began flexing its muscles by rejecting the postal privatization bills in 2005. At that time it prompted the dissolution of the lower house, and then it asserted its strength in legislative behavior after the DPJ took control of the upper house in 2007. Masuyama (2007, 5–7) shows that the probability of a hypothetical average prime minister resigning substantively increases once the public approval rating drops below 50 percent, and it is over 50 percent if the approval rating further decreases to around 35 percent.

Not only does a prime minister's survival depend on citizens' support, citizens' evaluations of the prime minister influence their voting preferences, and thus public opinion is crucial to prime ministers (Ikeda 2004; Krauss and Nyblade 2004; Kabashima and Imai 2001). Parties cannot do well anymore if they select leaders with only the factional balance or their traditional support base in mind; they must pay attention to the preferences of ordinary citizens.

In addition, trends that have long been recognized in U.S. politics are now more prominent in Japan: ratings are a key determinant of leader effectiveness and influence legislative priorities, general strategy, and ultimate success (Brace and Hinckley 1992; Kernell 1997; Newman 2002, 782).[1]

As we discuss in the next chapter, powers are now more concentrated in the prime minister's office. Prime ministers are able to influence policy, and the media can help this process by providing a route by which they can bypass recalcitrant party elements and appeal directly to the public for support. In this way, the media can help move politics from local clientelist practices to national programmatic politics in which the prime minister is

---

1. Eda Kenji, secretary to Prime Minister Hashimoto Ryutaro (1996–98), describes a similar situation in Japan: it was not until Hashimoto's ratings fell dramatically that Diet members were emboldened to criticize Hashimoto and denounce the administration's policies (Eda 2002, 14–15).

clearly associated with a policy platform and can be rewarded or punished at the ballot box. This can lead to greater citizen oversight of politics.

Using case studies of successful and failed reform proposals, Shinoda Tomohito (2000), a professor at the International University of Japan, provides an analytical framework for examining prime ministers' policy-making capacity. He shows that prime ministers can be effective, and identifies the legal and informal sources of power available to Japanese prime ministers. Shinoda's framework centers on institutional sources of power, but he argues that one of the major informal sources of power is the support of the public.[2] Based on his case studies of policymaking, Shinoda describes four types of leadership style among Japanese prime ministers. He characterizes prime ministers according to the sources of power they utilize in the policy process and labels the types the political insider, the grandstander, the kamikaze fighter, and the peace lover. Although Shinoda's book was published before Koizumi Junichiro became prime minister, Koizumi was clearly a grandstander: lacking internal sources of power, he sought external support from the public and the media.

In this chapter, we use Koizumi as a case study. Public ratings were a particularly important resource for Koizumi, since he lacked a stable factional base and was in a minority position ideologically within his own party. He needed the political capital that high ratings could provide, given that his party would not jettison a popular leader who could provide electoral benefits.

Citizen Approval

Koizumi did not mark the beginning of a new era in Japanese politics, but he is thus far an outlier in the trend of "presidentialization." Even compared with Nakasone, whose premiership was based on public support and who stressed strong leadership and even used words like "presidential prime minister," Koizumi was still unusual. We described in the last chapter how Koizumi needed to cement his position as party leader and did so

---

2. The other sources are having a power base within the ruling party; control over the bureaucracy; ties with the opposition parties; business support; and international reputation. He argues that because prime ministers need informal sources of power to utilize institutional sources of power their effectiveness varies depending on four somewhat broad categories: their background, level of experience, political skills, and personality.

with a strategy that won him increased media coverage. Here we look at the results of this strategy.

In stark contrast to the patterns found in other nations and among most previous and subsequent Japanese prime ministers, Koizumi enjoyed unprecedented levels of support throughout most of his tenure as prime minister.[3] His popularity peaked the month after he became prime minister, when 73 percent of the population supported his cabinet.[4] His ratings then declined, but the drop was followed by a remarkable recovery, and for most of his term in office, his average popularity level fluctuated around 48 percent (see figure 5.1). As such, Koizumi's ratings were well above the 36 percent average that post-1960 cabinets in Japan have endured.

How was Koizumi able to maintain such high approval ratings throughout most of his five-year tenure as prime minister of Japan?

We discussed the importance of politicians' media image and coverage in chapter 4. Here we look in more detail at the kinds of events and news coverage that improve popularity. In effect, we are asking: "Is all news good news?" We demonstrate that to halt the decline in their support, prime ministers must provide the media with the kinds of stories that they prefer, in short, a digestible series of stories of drama and conflict (Osaka 2006; Popkin 2006). Most analyses of approval ratings acknowledge that the media are the critical factor in transmitting information. Here we demonstrate that television exposure was directly associated with Koizumi's support ratings, but not all political events that the media cover are associated with increased approval ratings. While it is true that prime ministers need not be passive observers of their declining support, approval ratings are not easy to manipulate, and the strategies Koizumi used were not always successful.

Next, we briefly examine the effects of Koizumi's popularity on citizens' voting preferences in his first election as prime minister. We then describe the political events on which the media reported extensively and that pundits have assumed influenced Koizumi's ratings, before presenting quantitative analysis to show which events actually influenced public support.

---

3. Such monotonic declines in the cabinet approval rate are notable particularly for Tanaka Kakuei and Hosokawa Morihiro, who started their tenures with unusually high approval rates.

4. JiJi Press conducts monthly nationwide public opinion surveys that ask respondents whether or not they support the cabinet. Analysts typically view these as measures of support for the prime minister (Krauss and Nyblade 2004).

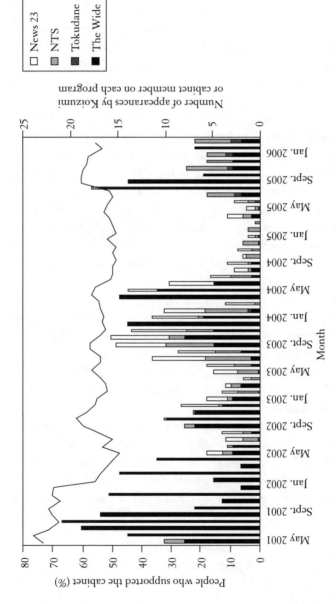

Figure 5.1. Koizumi's cabinet support and television appearances. Data compiled from data from JiJi Press and the Kabashima Seminar.

Prime Ministers and Citizens' Vote Choice

Initially, the media shared with citizens euphoria over Koizumi. But the media became more critical when his reform agenda stalled, before returning to more positive coverage once the reforms progressed. In the run-up to Koizumi's first election as LDP leader, citizens were enthusiastic about Koizumi and reporters were still positive and their output prolific.

Koizumi's popularity influenced the vote choice not only of LDP supporters, but also of supporters of the DPJ. We can gauge Koizumi's impact through examining "fixed-point" observations—repeated responses from the same voters—on their opinions and voting preferences using data from the Japan Election Survey II that we describe in appendix C. The vote in the 2001 upper house election can be broken down among three groups of voters (see table 5.1): (1) those who voted for the LDP in the 2000 lower house election, (2) those who voted for the DPJ on that occasion, and (3) those who did not vote then. The LDP had a high support-retention rate: more than four-fifths of those who voted for the party in the 2000 lower house election did so again the following year in the upper house election. By contrast, the DPJ's support-retention rate was a mere 45 percent, and a full quarter of those who voted for the DJP in 2000 switched to the LDP in 2001.[5]

The pie charts in figure 5.2 show the percentages of independents who voted for each party in the elections of 2000 and 2001. The LDP's vote share surged from 14 percent in 2000 to 25 percent in 2001, while the DPJ's vote fell from 37 percent to 28 percent. However, a number of independents who voted DJP in 2000 switched to the LDP in 2001, presumably because they approved of Koizumi.

In earlier research, I (Kabashima Ikuo) presented a basic model analyzing the vote choice of people who voted for one of the opposition parties or who abstained in the 2000 lower house election but switched to the LDP in the 2001 upper house election. It is clear that the change was largely due to Koizumi's personal popularity (Kabashima 2004, 362; see also Ikeda 2004).[6]

---

5. The LDP could have capitalized further on the "Koizumi effect" had they fielded more candidates: to avoid splitting their vote in multiseat constituencies, as they had in the 1998 upper house election, the LDP decided in general to field only one candidate. (This decision was made during Mori's unpopular tenure as prime minister.) This conservative strategy lost the LDP at least six seats (Kabashima 2001, 24–25).

6. The model suggests that the probability of voters switching to the LDP depended on their approval of the prime minister, on changes in people's feelings toward the LDP and the DPJ, and on voters' ideologies.

TABLE 5.1
Voters' Party Choice in the 2000 Lower House and 2001 Upper House Elections: LDP Retention versus DPJ Defection (percent)

	Party Voted for in 2001 (Upper House Election)							
	LDP	DPJ	Komeito	JCP	SDP	Liberal	Other	Abstained/ No Answer
Party voted for in 2000 (lower house election, PR portion)								
LDP	81.8	4.7	1.6	0.5	0.5	2.6	2.1	6.3
DPJ	25.0	44.9	4.0	5.1	5.1	6.8	2.8	6.2
Abstained	22.7	13.6	0.0	0.0	4.5	0.0	9.0	50.0

Source: JES II.
Note: The data show the percentage of people who voted for each party in the 2000 lower house election who also voted for a given party in the 2001 upper house election.

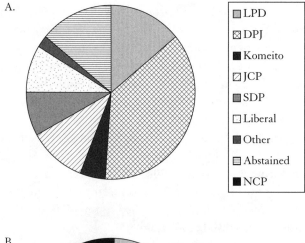

A.

LPD
DPJ
Komeito
JCP
SDP
Liberal
Other
Abstained
NCP

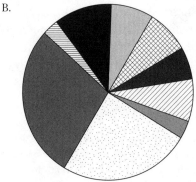

B.

Figure 5.2. The floating vote, 2000–2001, showing vote shares from the PR portion. A, vote choice of independents, lower house election 2000; B, vote choice of independents, upper house election 2001. JES II.

Approval-Enhancing and Approval-Diminishing Events

Koizumi skillfully blended an unconventional style with unconventional policies—a mutual reinforcing of style and substance that appealed to the public. New York University political theorist Bernard Manin notes that in contemporary democracies, representatives are elected on the basis of "image." He points out that voting on the basis of image is sometimes understood to be superficial and devoid of political content—as opposed to voting on the basis of detailed knowledge of policy proposals—but, in fact, images are not free of political content (Manin 1997, 227).

Yet style and public relations alone were unlikely to sustain Koizumi's approval ratings over the long run. Some previous cross-national research, particularly on U.S. presidential approval, indicates that three broad categories of events influence ratings: peace, prosperity, and domestic tranquility (see Ostrom and Simon 1988, 1100). Some theorists describe these very broad classes as "levers" that are available to leaders to influence support. Ostrom and Simon (1989, 365) offer a brief review of this literature, pointing to research that highlights the use of such strategies as political drama, television, foreign travel, and macroeconomic management as "approval-enhancing" events, whereas events that increase "doubt, dissatisfaction, or disappointment," such as allegations of wrongdoing, are "approval-diminishing" events (1989, 365). Still other researchers contest the efficacy of these strategies, claiming that, at least in the United States, presidents are virtually unable to maintain support (Lowi 1985).

Commentators have assumed that various events within these broad categories would similarly influence Koizumi's approval ratings.

Political Drama

With his flair for public relations, Koizumi made Japanese politics exciting again. His promises to "smash" the LDP astonished his own party and earned him the support of citizens who had turned against the LDP. Koizumi dramatized his beleaguered position within the LDP, managing to position himself as the standard-bearer of the reform camp who was seeking to promote the interests of the electorate and who was fighting the self-serving politics of the old guard. The press saw him as an Oda Nobunaga–like figure. Nobunaga, born into the family of a minor sixteenth-century provincial lord, became a brilliant, brutal military tactician who decimated his enemies and paved the way for the unification of Japan.

Prosperity: Dramatizing the Economy

During the Heisei recession, successive cabinets rolled out their suggested stimulus packages or structural reform plans: a reform package was nothing new. What was different was the presentation of Koizumi's policies via the media. Koizumi proposed neoliberal economic reforms that were underpinned by an anti–status quo orientation. He made clear that the public would experience hardship in the short term, and he constantly used the sound bite "no pain, no gain" (so much so that during the campaign period alone, Asahi News group articles on Koizumi carried 122 mentions of the word "pain"). To make his rhetoric plausible, Koizumi repeatedly claimed that not only the general public but also the LDP, and the LDP's support base, would suffer.

After one year in office, with no miraculous cure for the ailing economy and in the absence of the promised economic progress, Koizumi himself seemed like old news, and support for his cabinet fell (see figure 5.1). The cabinet's support rate plunged sharply from February to June 2002, particularly after Koizumi removed the popular and outspoken Tanaka Makiko from her position as foreign minister. Her dismissal uncorked people's simmering dissatisfaction with the prime minister, who had made little progress on his promised agenda. In chapter 4, we discussed Uesugi's (2006) claim that the media restrained themselves from reporting extensively on Tanaka Makiko's various controversies because she was so popular and the media did not want to alienate their audience/readers.

Diplomatic Initiatives

Particularly during the early years, it was difficult for Koizumi to focus solely on structural reform, as he allowed himself to be sidetracked by the thorny task of getting some controversial legislation through parliament. A package of bills approved by the cabinet on April 16, 2002, giving the national government broader powers to respond to armed attacks on Japan, attracted particularly strong opposition, since it was the first of this type of legislation in the postwar era, indicative of a new stage in Japan's security-policy debate.

In general, Koizumi tried to take the initiative with "leader-led diplomacy" (*shuno gaiko*) or "*Kantei gaiko*" (Cabinet Office–led diplomacy), as the press frequently described it at the time. This strategy emphasizes meetings between leaders and solving problems at the political level, rather than delegating responsibility to the Foreign Ministry as "Foreign Ministry–led diplomacy" (*Gaimusho gaiko*) (see Iijima, 2007). This suited

Koizumi's personality and is also obviously an attention-grabbing strategy that increases the possibility of media coverage.

Against the background of falling public approval and watered-down economic reform, Koizumi made the stunning announcement that he would travel to the Democratic People's Republic of Korea for a historic summit in September 2002. He became the first Japanese prime minister to travel to North Korea and meet Kim Jong Il. The declaration from the summit announced the commencement of normalization talks between the two countries (as part of this, Japan would provide economic assistance in return for North Korean compliance on missile- and nuclear-related issues). More astonishing, though, was North Korea's astounding admission that it had actually abducted Japanese citizens in the 1970s and early 1980s and their apology for doing so.

Suspicious disappearances and later testimony from North Korean agents had led the Japanese government to suspect North Korea of abducting Japanese people, charges that the North Korean government had denied for years. One month after the summit, five of those who had been abducted were repatriated to Japan, leaving behind their Korean-born children and one victim's American husband. It was not until July 2004 that one of the families was reunited.

Koizumi's support ratings improved, along with the outpouring of public sympathy for the victims and their families and heightened anger at the North Korean government that perpetrated the kidnappings.[7] For the two years following Koizumi's first summit with North Korea, the abduction issue dominated Japanese politics and diplomacy; the government gave priority to bringing back the victims and to obtaining information about deceased victims. Abe Shinzo, Koizumi's successor (see chapter 6), had thrust himself into the limelight on the abduction issue. He worked on this issue for several years and traveled to Pyongyang with Koizumi as deputy cabinet secretary. The media portrayed Abe as a tough negotiator who refused North Korean demands to return the abductees to North Korea, as had been arranged, once they arrived in Japan.

But the issue was not straightforward: the public was reluctant to support normalization of relations without fully understanding the fate of the abducted Japanese. Kato Koichi, then secretary-general of the LDP (and former chief cabinet secretary and secretary of defense), claims that

7. They were apparently kidnapped to steal their identities, to train North Korean agents, and to marry members of the Red Army Faction who had hijacked a flight in 1970 and some of whom were still living in North Korea (Ministry of Foreign Affairs 2008).

the wide shows influenced policy toward North Korea. He claims that the normalization of relations between Japan and North Korea could not progress because the wide shows opposed normalization in the absence of a satisfactory solution to the abduction problem (Taniguchi 2004). The Japanese government has identified another seventeen people whom it believes the North Koreans abducted and failed to provide adequate information about (Ministry of Foreign Affairs 2008).

Public support for the Koizumi administration at that time may also have stemmed from the failure of the DPJ to convince the public that they had a competent or equally charismatic alternative to Koizumi. The public was still unsure of the inexperienced DPJ and whether or not it was competent to govern. The LDP, too, lacked an alternative to Koizumi; on the LDP side, the young reform-minded LDP politicians were relatively inexperienced.

Public support played a crucial role in Koizumi's victory in the LDP presidential election in the fall of 2003. The general election loomed large in the minds of the LDP Diet members, particularly since in recent elections public support for the LDP leader influenced voting preferences. LDP politicians were keenly aware that their own seats would be jeopardized if the party failed to elect a popular leader. Following Koizumi's re-selection, the Koizumi "magic" returned. The levels of media exposure peaked during this period. Until June 2004 more people consistently approved than disapproved of the cabinet. Koizumi was successful in maintaining his image as an unorthodox, unusual leader of the LDP, particularly compared with most past LDP presidents. Even though his attacks against the "the forces of resistance" gradually subsided, his approval rate remained high enough for him to keep his LDP opponents in check.

Allegations of Wrongdoing versus Political Drama

Ironically, the media broke the story of a scandal involving politicians not paying pension contributions (the *nenkin mondai*) as politicians debated revising the Pension Law in April and May 2004. The scandal involved an astonishing number of politicians who had not consistently paid their pension contributions. From mid-2004 onward, Koizumi's approval ratings went into free fall, despite significant economic improvements. This was partly attributable to the DPJ's new leader. Okada Katsuya was selected to replace Kan Naoto (who had resigned over unpaid pension contributions), and the public and the media reacted positively, approving of Okada's proclaimed straightforward political attitudes, integrity, and photogenic qualities.

The most devastating discovery was that Koizumi himself had not consistently paid his pension contributions, which prompted a media attack. Koizumi tried to downplay the accusations, arguing that at the time it was not mandatory for politicians to join the pension program. On the same day that Koizumi admitted to a period of nonpayment, he made the dramatic announcement that he intended to visit North Korea for a second time. A majority of citizens approved of Koizumi's decision. The decision had clearly been in the pipeline for some time, but both the timing of the announcement and the timing of the second summit in May 2004, two months before the upper house election and in the midst of the pension scandal, prompted some critics to describe the summit as a diversionary tactic.

This incident demonstrates the limits to the use of "levers" to influence public support. Despite the second trip to Pyongyang, support for the administration continued its descent for the rest of the year. The North Korean issue temporarily eclipsed the pension scandal in the media, and when the Korean-born children and the American husband of one of the repatriated victims were released (supposedly temporarily) one month later, Koizumi's popularity rose again. However, feelings were mixed: according to a survey conducted by the *Asahi Shimbun,* about 67 percent of voters approved of Koizumi's trip, but at the same time, 61 percent of the respondents opposed Japan's plan to provide humanitarian aid to North Korea.

In the House of Councillors' election held on July 11, 2004, the DPJ won a majority of the seats contested, sweeping the urban areas (although the LDP still held a majority of seats overall). LDP support continued to decline and stood at less than 36 percent at the end of the year. In early 2005, however, LDP support rebounded, and it remained fairly steady until August 2005, helped by the DPJ failing to capitalize on the initial appeal of their leader and to be an effective opposition (see chapter 7).

Diplomatic Anti-Initiatives

Each year during his prime ministership, Koizumi made highly publicized visits to Yasukuni Shrine, the shrine that commemorates Japan's war dead and, more controversially, enshrines class A war criminals. Some citizens strongly objected to Koizumi's visits as violating the separation of state and religion and took Koizumi to court.[8] For some citizens in Asian nations,

---

8. In a survey conducted by the *Yomiuri Shimbun* on August 9, 2006, 50% of the respondents opposed Koizumi's visits, whereas 40% supported them.

the shrine symbolizes Japan's militaristic past, and the Chinese and South Korean governments in particular strongly objected to Koizumi's visits. He brushed off this criticism as "none of other countries' business." His continued visits despite objections led to strained relations between Japan and other Asian countries.

More Political Drama

As part of economic restructuring, the Koizumi cabinet proposed a series of postal privatization bills that squeaked through the lower house on July 7, 2005, with thirty-seven members of the LDP voting against the bills. Indicative of the coming drama, the day before the upper house vote, Koizumi dramatically pronounced to former prime minister Mori Yoshiro "[Postal privatization] is my belief. I am even ready to be killed [for that]." The bills failed to make it through the upper house, galvanizing Koizumi for a fight. He dissolved the lower house, since the upper house cannot be dissolved, and called an election.

Koizumi was determined to fight the election on the issue of postal reform. In what was the most exciting campaign in decades, he denied party endorsement to the LDP politicians who had voted against the bills and parachuted in hand-picked warriors to battle the antireformists (the media labeled them "assassins"). Many of his "warriors" were attractive and slick in front of the camera: some were high-profile women; most were relatively young; some were celebrities and other successful non-politicians. They included Katayama Satsuki, a former winner of the Miss Tokyo University beauty pageant who had become a bureaucrat in the Ministry of Finance; former cabinet minister Koike Yuriko, a household name and former news anchorwoman, and Inoguchi Kuniko, a university professor and frequent television guest. These pro-reform candidates were dubbed "Koizumi's Children."[9]

Resorting to his penchant for drama, Koizumi portrayed the election as a clash between good (assassins/reformers) and evil (rebels/antireformists). The election became known as the Koizumi Theater. Koizumi successfully set the agenda of the election, asking the public whether they supported reform (privatization of the post office); a vote for Koizumi and

9. 73 of Koizumi's protégés ran in the 2009 lower house election, 65 in single-seat constituencies and 8 in proportional representation blocs, with another 4 running for other parties or independently. Only 10 managed to hang onto their seats, 3 of which were in SMDs (*Mainichi Shimbun* 2009b).

the LDP became a vote for reform, a vote for change, rather than for the status quo.

The opposition failed to undermine this agenda and failed to provide the media with a more interesting story, so Koizumi and his assassins dominated the media's coverage of the election. As Osaka Iwao, Rikkyo University expert on politics and the media, points out in his analysis of the 2005 election, the mass media, particularly the wide shows, considered conflict (and war) to be compelling stories—commodities that interest the consumer. Public interestedness, as measured by ratings (that is, sales) influences the duration and placement of the coverage, and in their increased coverage of politics during the 2001 to 2005 period the wide shows focused on war, conflict, and danger. The media would not fail to report on postal reform and the ensuing campaign, since it was presented as a "civil war" (Osaka 2006, 14–15).

Koizumi was a prime example of the media being carried away by populist politicians, unusual tactics, and complex policies that can undermine their role as watchdog. Uesugi (2006) claims that Koizumi shocked most journalists when he dissolved the lower house: they understood the regular political games, but when Koizumi did not play by the rules, this confused them and allowed him to get the upper hand, forcing the journalists to follow the frenzy, rather than stay in control. Uesugi also says that he himself focused on the theatrical elements of Koizumi's tenure, such as Koizumi's battle with the old guard, and not on the policies, because he didn't fully understand the nitty-gritty of the policies of structural reform.

The LDP won a huge share of the seats. As discussed earlier, voters cast two ballots, one in their single-seat constituency and the other for a political party (the PR portion). Although the LDP's seat share massively increased, the LDP's share of the popular vote increased from 44 percent in 2003 to 48 percent in the single-member districts, and from 35 percent to 38 percent in the PR vote (see Krauss and Pekkanen 2008).[10]

The lower house election of 2005 was Koizumi's last chance to make his mark and avoid being dismissed as a lame duck prime minister. He

---

10. The LDP apparently did much better than it expected, and some of the candidates they placed toward the bottom of the PR lists were not well vetted. Sugimura Taizo, for example, actually won a seat for the Minami-Kanto bloc. The media had a field day over his excited comments about the perks available for politicians: "A big apartment, I can hardly wait!" "A Diet member's salary is 25,000,000 yen!" He also expressed happiness at being able to go to a high-class restaurant for the first time and being able to afford the BMW he had wanted. After the LDP executives criticized him, he publicly apologized for his "immature and irresponsible" comments.

had accomplished some of what he set out to do, but some of his reforms had been diluted and others were nonstarters; and, although the economy was picking up, support for his cabinet was declining. Koizumi claimed to want to change the LDP, but in the previous four years he had done little to increase female representation or to include more younger Diet members. He used the "assassin" candidates as a tactic to regain popularity. Cynics argue that postal reform was only a tool; of course he wanted to pass his reforms, but more than that, he wanted to appear revolutionary.

We tested whether increased media exposure was associated with higher levels of support for Koizumi, using data from the JiJi Press, which conducts surveys on cabinet support during the second week of each month, taking into account political and economic factors that may increase support levels.[11]

Television Exposure

We examined whether the number of times each month Koizumi or his cabinet were featured on *NTS*, *News23*, *Tokudane* [Scoop], and *The Wide* (two each of the most popular hard- and soft-news programs) was associated with cabinet support. We used these programs as a proxy for overall levels of television exposure and included hard- and soft-news programs, since they are reach a wider audience than, for example, front-page news in a national daily newspaper.[12]

In addition to television exposure, we took into account political events that occurred each month. Most cross-national models of approval include important events, but there is little agreement as to what constitutes "important." Broadly following Ostrom and Simon's (1985) approach, we identified events that were "specific, dramatic and sharply focused," directly connected to Koizumi, and the object of extensive media coverage

11. The respondents are drawn from representative samples of adults, with sample sizes of approximately 1,400. The surveys use face-to-face interviews and ask respondents whether or not they support the cabinet. We examined the period from May 2001 to March 2006. We estimated a time series regression model. Examination of the residuals of the dependent variable demonstrated evidence of autocorrelation, in particular, the first lag was significant. (Unsurprisingly, the Box-Ljung Q test was also significant, indicating that we cannot reject the null hypothesis of no autocorrelation.) To correct for this first-order autocorrelation, we used an ARIMA estimator.

12. These data were gathered from the television guide of the morning edition of the *Asahi Shimbun* by the Kabashima Seminar (*zemi*) 2005–6.

(Newman, 2002).[13] As Ostrom and Simon put it, "a given performance dimension will enter into the calculus of support only if there is some reason for citizens to notice" (Ostrom and Simon 1985, 337).

We tested whether three categories of political events influenced support ratings: significant Japanese involvement with foreign nations (both diplomatic and military); selected significant domestic events; and a significant event relating to the prime minister's integrity. Specifically, we looked at Koizumi's Yasukuni visits; the return of the abductees; the North Korea summits; Japanese troops joining the Iraq force; Tanaka Makiko fired; elections; the September 2005 election campaign; and Koizumi admitting to not paying pension contributions.

So that the models are not biased in favor of political factors or media exposure, we also included economic indicators that the media routinely report, specifically the unemployment rate and the consumer price index. Most previous research had found that economic factors do not influence political support in Japan (Anderson and Ishii 1997; Reed and Brunk 1984). However, the public may have held Koizumi to different standards and used economic factors to evaluate him, since, as we discussed earlier, neoliberal economic reform was a fundamental part of Koizumi's rhetoric (see this chapter's appendix 5.1 for more details about the variables).

Our findings indicate that higher rates of media exposure of the Koizumi cabinet are associated with increased popularity, even after taking into account the effects of political and economic variables. The months in which elections were held, Koizumi's visits to Yasukuni Shrine, and firing Tanaka Makiko all lowered Koizumi's ratings. Other political issues were not so straightforward and show the limits to prime ministers' ability to manipulate support. We expected the North Korean summits and their outcome, the return of the abductees, to produce a "rally round the flag" effect for Koizumi, but the reality was more complex. Although public opinion surveys showed support for the summits, the second was widely seen as a diversionary tactic, occurring in tandem with the disclosure of nonpayment of pension contributions. The signs of these coefficients are in the expected direction, but they are not significant (see table 5.2).

The clearest approval-enhancing event was the rejection of the postal reform bills by the upper house and Koizumi's reaction of dissolving the

13. We do not view all citizens as equally aware, interested in, or attentive to the news, but the available data do not allow more nuanced analysis. Including only events that have been extensively covered also increases the likelihood that citizens will include the outcome of the event in evaluations of the prime minister's performance.

TABLE 5.2
The Media and Koizumi's Support

Independent Variables	Cabinet Support
Media exposure	0.056**
	[0.028]
Yasukuni Shrine	−4.865*
	[1.743]
Tanaka fired$_{t-1}$	−20.868*
	[3.824]
Abductees return	8.276
	[10.008]
N. Korea summits	4.563
	[6.191]
Join Iraq force$_{t-1}$	−8.667
	[29.909]
Pension nonpayment	−2.424
	[56.575]
September 2005	12.452*
	[4.831]
Elections	−9.159*
	[3.267]
Duration	−0.04
	[0.044]
Cabinet support$_{t-1}$	0.926*
	[0.043]
Unemployment	−1.103
	[1.295]
CPI	0.699
	[1.207]
Constant	−59.671
	[118.870]
Sigma	2.726
	[.313]
Log likelihood	−140.60
Observations	58

Notes: Cell entries are coefficients from ARIMA error process with standard errors in brackets. The dependent variable is citizen support for the cabinet.
* significant at 1%; ** significant at 5%
We code only for the number of appearances.

lower house and basing the ensuing election campaign on this issue in August and September 2005. This was a huge boost to Koizumi's popularity. The public was mobilized around an issue when it was presented coherently and dramatically.

Koizumi did not lose support during his tenure (the variable that represents length of time Koizumi spent in office is not significant). He did, however, in common with many governments, lose support in elections after his initial victory (with the exception of the September 2005 election).

Public support was particularly important for Koizumi because he lacked support within his own party; he had to maintain public approval to bypass the antireformists in his own party who opposed his policies but would not jettison a popular leader. To maintain public support, he used various strategies to increase his coverage in the media. But there are limits to the levers available to Japanese prime ministers for generating popularity. Koizumi hoped to shore up his flagging popularity with visits to North Korea and bringing home kidnapped citizens, but the public was not fully convinced by this ambiguous issue. He was much more successful in portraying himself as fighting the old guard in a "struggle" that culminated in turning the 2005 election into an attention-grabbing "theater."

Postal reform and the 2005 election were of dramatic, but transient, significance to his ratings.[14] Koizumi was fortunate in being able to frame a policy issue as a struggle, to which the public responded, but his successors were not as astute—or fortunate—in doing so. Politicians cannot be sure that the issues they choose will resonate with the electorate; instead, they become involved in a constant process of trial and error.

When we look at the economy, despite Koizumi's strong focus on economic reform, neither the consumer price index nor the unemployment rates contributed to Koizumi's support. Citizens may have continued their past processes of attitude formation, in which they did not punish the LDP electorally when the economy performed poorly. Although Koizumi stressed economic recovery as central to his agenda, economic recovery as an evaluative tool is based on the assumption that citizens use their own preferences to judge leaders and that such evaluations are a function of a comparison between expected and actual performance (Ostrom and Simon 1985, 336). Underpinning this model is the assumption that citizens are clear as to their own preferences, can link these preferences to economic performance, and are clear as to where responsibility for the economy lies. In this case, it was not clear who was responsible for the economy, and this worked in Koizumi's favor.[15] Koizumi had promised voters that "pain" would accompany reform, and thus he avoided

14. Carmines and Stimson describe such a pattern as an "impulse-decay model" in their study of race as an issue in U.S. politics, suggesting that it is possible for issues to have a short, but powerful, influence on the political system (Carmines and Stimson 1989, 139).

15. Powell and Whitten (1993) describe the disconnectedness between the economy and voting preferences as a lack of "clarity of responsibility." Although Japan does not have all of the characteristics Powell and Whitten identify, the diffuse responsibility they point to is particularly prominent in Japan. In nations where responsibility is less clear, incumbent governments are less likely to be punished or rewarded by voters for the economy. Koizumi is a more specific case than are the cases quantified by Powell and Whitten's index, but the concept encompasses this situation.

responsibility when the economy failed to improve. In addition, Koizumi's much-publicized struggles to enact his reform program meant that initial delays in enacting reforms were portrayed as the responsibility of the old guard. As long as he could remind citizens that he alone was not to blame, it was less likely that voters would enact a simple reward-punishment scenario in which they credit the government when the economy performs well and blame the government when the economy performs poorly. By stressing his predicament, Koizumi was able to further diffuse responsibility in a system in which responsibility had not even been strongly allocated to prime ministers in the first place. But when the economy did improve, citizens did not assign credit to Koizumi either. Overall, our results fit with contextual studies that suggest that the broader political-institutional environment is crucial in influencing whether the public attaches credit or blame for the economy and votes accordingly (Hellwig 2001, 1144).

Appendix 5.1

Details of Variables

	Minimum	Maximum	Mean	N
Cabinet support	34	78	47.7	58
Media exposure	2	74	27.3	58
Elections	0	1	.07	58
Yasukuni Shrine	0	1	.09	58
Tanaka fired	0	1	.02	58
Abductees return	0	1	.18	58
North Korea summits	0	1	.03	58
Pension nonpayment	0	1	.02	58
Join Iraq force	0	1	.02	58
September 2005	0	1	.02	58
Unemployment	4.0	5.8	4.94	58
CPI	97.4	99.6	98.2	58
Duration	2	59	30.5	58

Notes: We created a series of dummy variables to operationalize the events: elections (1 = election in lower or upper house, 0 if otherwise, does not include September 2005 election); Yasukuni visits (1 = months Koizumi visited the shrine, 0 if otherwise); Tanaka fired (1 = February 2002, 0 if otherwise); abductees return (1 = months abductees returned to Japan, 0 if otherwise); North Korea summits (1 = Koizumi visits North Korea, 0 if otherwise); pension nonpayment (1 = month Koizumi admitted to not fully paying pensions contributions, 0 if otherwise); join Iraq force (1 = month cabinet announces Japan to join U.S.-led multinational force in Iraq, 0 if otherwise); September campaign (1 = September 2005, 0 if otherwise). The variables that represent Tanaka being fired and Japan joining the forces in Iraq were lagged by one month since the announcements were made after the surveys were conducted. We include a lagged dependent variable on the right-hand side to capture the inertia component of approval (Baum and Kernell 2001, 217) and a variable to measure the duration of Koizumi's tenure in office to capture the conventional wisdom that governments lose support the longer they remain in office.

6

REPRESENTATION AND POLICYMAKING UNDER LDP ADMINISTRATIONS IN THE POST-1955 SYSTEM

By the beginning of the 1990s, citizens were angry, and politicians themselves, perhaps fearing for their own livelihoods, enacted a whole series of reforms that strengthened their position in policymaking and at the same time gave citizens more oversight over politicians' actions. In this chapter we examine these reforms to understand whether the reforms have influenced the quality of representation.

As a whole, the reforms enacted throughout the 1990s are so extensive that Takenaka Harukata, a professor at Tokyo's National Graduate Institute for Policy Studies, describes them as a process of "democratic deepening" that has completely transformed Japan's system of public management and governance (Takenaka 2003). Professor Gregory Noble of the University of Tokyo's Social Science Institute concurs:

> Institutional reforms swept over the electoral system, the operation of the cabinet, economic management and such administrative practices as information openness, administrative procedures, and privatization. Contrary to widespread impressions, changes in institutions and procedures smoothed the way for measurable changes in economic management. (Noble 2005, 1)

The laws enacted included the Administrative Procedural Law (1993) that requires the government to open the process of administrative guidance—the informal directives issued by government ministries—to the public, thus increasing transparency and the potential for public oversight of governance. The Revised Political Funds Regulation Law (1994) aims to clean up campaign financing practices by introducing public financing for political parties and restricting the sources and sizes of private contributions that parties can accept. Laws to promote decentralization (1995; 1999) devolve administration of social policy to the local level and reform local-national financial relations. The Non-Profit Organization Law (1998) makes it easier for citizens to form NPOs, which—coupled with the increased freedom of information—facilitates greater citizen oversight of the government and increases the potential for accountability and fairer representation. Laws that further increase citizen oversight of politics include the Information Disclosure Law (1998) that stipulates that the government must disclose official documents allowing citizens access to information to enable them to monitor the processes of government. In addition, increasing access to information for those outside the compartmentalized policy domains may improve the quality of policymaking. Before the law, much work on gathering information and conducting research was completed by the *shingikai* (advisory councils) and bureaucrats, who drafted virtually all reports. Now outsiders have increased access to the work of the councils and council members increasingly draft their own reports; the minutes and reports of almost all councils are readily available on the internet (see Noble 2005). Further strengthening politicians' say in policymaking, the Revised National Administrative Law (1999) and the Revised Diet Law (1999) shift the prerogative of policy proposal and formation to politicians and away from bureaucrats.

Prime Minister Hashimoto Ryutaro (1996–98), a long-term supporter of reform who had been instrumental in the Nakasone reforms, introduced reforms of the administrative system that took effect in January 2001. Administrative reform was the cornerstone of his broader reform program, since the other reforms were predicated on a reduction and reorganization of bureaucratic power (Bevacqua 1997; Ministry of Finance 1997). Hashimoto sought public backing for his reforms by stressing the importance of prime ministerial leadership and dramatizing the situation with his now-famous comment that he would accomplish reform even if he became "engulfed in flames." The legislation decreased the number of ministries by more than a quarter in an attempt to increase coordination and to reduce the "sectionalism" or turf battles that impeded smooth policymaking. However, Hashimoto was forced to compromise on some aspects of his bureaucratic reorganization proposals, and skeptics wondered if reducing the number of ministries would make any difference.

Shimizu Masato (2005) argues that the movement to create a genuinely stronger cabinet grew out of the failed attempts of the Hosokawa and

Murayama administrations, when the prime ministers were thwarted in their attempts to change policy and top bureaucrat Ishihara Nobuo (then vice cabinet secretary) was able to dominate the cabinet. Nakasone had previously attempted to reinforce the Cabinet Office by establishing two deliberative councils within the cabinet—one for domestic affairs and the other for foreign policy. These councils proved insufficient largely due to bureaucratic sectionalism and the desire of the bureaucracies—who dispatch staff to the councils—to protect their own turf. At the same time that he reduced the number of ministries, Hashimoto strengthened the legal authority and staff of the prime minister by expanding the Cabinet Office and clarifying its role. The Cabinet Office and Cabinet Secretariat were increased in size, and the prime minister became able to hire staff from outside the bureaucracies.[1] Changes firmly placed the prime minister and Cabinet Secretariat in control of the ministries and agencies and clarified the prerogative of the prime minister to direct meetings and the operations of the cabinet, thus reducing ministerial sway.

In the Diet, instead of bureaucrats responding on behalf of ministers, ministers themselves are now expected to master policy and answer questions. The prime minister, too, was not spared: the reforms introduced Question Time in which the opposition parties confront the prime minister in the Diet forcing him to defend his policies and his party.

Crucially, the reforms created four *shingikai* within the Cabinet Office—"super-*shingikai*," as Gregory Noble dubs these councils—the most important of which, the Council on Economic and Fiscal Policy (CEFP), has the prerogative to set the direction of the budget and economic policy (Noble 2005). The number of political appointees in each ministry—which used to be limited to two—was increased, strengthening the potential for political oversight of the bureaucracies. The system of vice ministers was revised to increase political control over the ministries and give younger politicians an opportunity to increase their knowledge and skills (Takenaka 2002). Up to two junior ministers can be appointed in each ministry (and six in the cabinet). Hashimoto also began the practice of appointing policy aides in addition to secretaries (Nakami 2003).[2]

---

1. Noble (2005) rejects criticism that the provisions of the reforms were not used. On the contrary, in the first few years of the new system alone, thirty-nine people joined the Cabinet Office from the private sector, think tanks, and academia (five more joined the Cabinet Secretariat), and most of these were in key positions.

2. Before Hashimoto, other prime ministers appointed what amounted to policy aides, but they were not official aide positions.

The changes to the policy-making apparatus now mean that prime ministers have the tools available to push through their own agendas, if they are policy entrepreneurs. Prime minister–led reforms provide the tools for strong prime ministers to carve roles for themselves and carry out their agendas in a top-down fashion, should they choose to do so. If this is the case, public support for policies can be crucial and can tie the hands of opponents and allow these policy entrepreneurs the space to succeed. When a prime minister has no policy agenda, the system reverts to its default mode (as described in chapter 2) in which policymaking is left to the *seisaku zoku* (policy tribes) and the bureaucrats.

Even before the reforms, in addition to creating new councils (and in other cases, consolidating existing councils), reformist prime ministers accomplished their goals by using the *shingikai* in new ways. During the 1955 system, most prime ministers did not have a strong role in policy-making, but some were able to set the overall direction of policy and others were policy entrepreneurs who were able to push through major reforms through a combination of reforming the system, creatively exploiting existing institutions, and gaining public support. Nakasone and Hashimoto both did so and were able to achieve major policy change. As we saw in chapter 2, Nakasone privatized major government corporations, deregulated the telecommunications market, and tried to delegate some responsibilities for social service provision to the private sphere. Hashimoto proposed six major reforms: administrative, fiscal, economic, financial, social security, and educational (the *rokudai kaikaku,* or the six big reforms). Noble (2005) describes how Hashimoto (like Nakasone) turned many *shingikai* attached to Japan's ministries that had previously been bastions of bureaucratic rule and reliable defenders of the status quo into centers for the promotion of neoliberal reform. They did so by changing the membership of some *shingikai* to include reformist academics, who then helped to marginalize old-style bureaucrats, and by selectively bypassing or preempting nonsupportive ministerial-level *shingikai* (Noble 2005, 9). Hashimoto, Hosokawa, and Koizumi actually headed crucial *shingikai* themselves. As we discuss later, the Hashimoto administration began decreasing Fiscal Investment and Loan Program (FILP) expenditures via recommendations from *shingikai,* and Koizumi accelerated the process. In 1996 Hashimoto created the Administrative Reform Council, an executive body whose purpose was to advise on reform (its members were from the business world, labor leaders, academics, and bureaucrats from major ministries) under his direct supervision. Hashimoto and other reformist politicians were very involved in the council's deliberations.

The Administrative Reform Council recommended various measures to strengthen politicians' authority vis à vis the bureaucrats, and in doing so it provoked an uproar from *zoku* politicians and bureaucrats (Kawabata 2008). Koizumi used CEFP recomendations as the basis for reform in many different areas (Amyx 2004).

Some analysts assume that citizens have a very limited role in this system, with the government making policy in what they perceive to be the national interest. Yet policymakers are often acutely aware of public opinion. Policy entrepreneurial prime ministers need to get public backing for controversial reforms, either by mobilizing opinion or by incorporating existing demands into policy formulation. The profound changes in welfare policymaking, for example, are guided to some extent by citizens' preferences. Against the background of cutbacks and Japan's economic slump, on April 1, 2000, Japan started "the biggest and most radical program of public, mandatory long-term care insurance (LTCI) in the world.... Japan has moved decisively toward 'socialization of care' for the frail elderly" (Campbell and Ikegami 2000, 27). Japan's public mandatory long-term care insurance program has generous benefits (all delivered in the form of services, not cash) that covers 90 percent of need.[3]

In formulating the policy, policymakers were highly concerned about public opinion: they worried that voters might object to paying a new social insurance premium, and in the end this resulted in various compromises to the proposed policy. An element of consumer choice is built in: consumers can select the services and providers they want, including for-profit companies. But, on the other hand, the policy was not exactly what the public wanted: public opinion polls showed that people wanted cash allowances for family care, but policymakers rejected this (Campbell and Ikegami 2000). Even expanding welfare provisions was not enough to save the LDP: at the turn of the century the LDP's popularity was at rock bottom.

In 2001 Koizumi took the helm of a deeply unpopular party. Gaining the support of the public was an overriding concern for him. To achieve his policy objectives, he had to overcome resistance from his own party and overcome the dynamics of the Liberal Democratic Party. Even though the Cabinet Office had been strenghtened considerably, its relative weakness

3. The long-term care insurance program covers both institutional and community-based care giving. Everyone age forty and older pays premiums. Everyone age sixty-five and older is eligible for benefits based strictly on physical and mental disability (see Campbell and Ikegami 2000).

could have allowed the antireform bureaucrats and politicians the upper hand in policymaking. Koizumi's neoliberal reforms pitted him against Diet members in his party who relied on the traditional pork-based machine politics. Koizumi was heir to the Kishi-Fukuda-Abe line of LDP leaders, who are ideologically different from the classic rural-oriented, social democratic, and redistributive LDP line epitomized by Tanaka Kakuei described in chapter 2.

The ideological line that Koizumi inherited has both a market-oriented and a nationalistic component, but Koizumi chose to devote most of his energies to the domestic arena, pressing for market-oriented reforms. The international component focused on independence from the United States, national security, and a greater role for Japan in international affairs.[4] Some, but not all, of these tendencies manifested themselves in Koizumi's "fighting diplomacy."[5] Prominent examples of this were Koizumi's dispatching the Self-Defense Forces to Iraq and brushing off criticism of his controversial visits to Yasukuni Shrine, which enraged China and South Korea. This situation was so serious that after Koizumi stepped down, many believed his successors needed to repair relations with Asian countries.

During the initial phases of Koizumi's first administration he was hampered by a stagnating economy and declining public support. Commentators agree that during the first few years of his administration, reform was minimal. Aurelia George Mulgan (2002), a professor at the University of New South Wales and long-term expert on Japanese politcs, writing one year into Koizumi's administration, dubbed Koizumi's reform effort "Japan's failed revolution" in a book with that title. Koizumi was trapped in a vicious cycle; he was hampered by the so-called forces of resistance and forced to water down some of his policies. Through this process Koizumi—who came on the scene promising to do away with old-style LDP dealings—was becoming more LDP-like, thus further reducing his support among the public. Koizumi's falling support ratings put fresh wind in the sails of the old guard, forcing him to bow further to some of the demands of the politicians and leaving him unable to push radical

4. Koizumi made many trips abroad. For a description of Koizumi's official visits abroad and meetings with leaders from various countries, see Iijima Isao's (2007) *Records of Koizumi Diplomacy.*

5. This description became a buzzword after *Yomiuri Shimbun* political reporters in 2006 published a book that became a best-seller, entitled *Gaiko Kenka ni Shita Otoko* (The man who turned diplomacy into fighting), their take on Koizumi's record.

policies through the legislature. The demands continued despite the fact that continuing economic problems meant the development and redistribution policies on which LDP Diet members relied were less tenable.

Reactions from the LDP antireformers and Koizumi's responses demonstrate how acrimonious the battle for reform was and clearly illustrate the opposing traditions within the LDP. Former party secretary-general Nonaka Hiromu and former Policy Affairs Research Council chair Kamei Shizuka were central in the anti-Koizumi movement and firmly part of the redistributive tradition in LDP politics. Nonaka blasted Koizumi's neoconservative policies as the "politics of the law of the jungle" that let the weak die while only the strong survive. He decried the general feeling that "this is only natural and proper" and the belief that it would lead to a bright future, stating that "human society must be based on equality. It is only when this premise is accepted that fair competition becomes possible" (see Kabashima 2002).

Kamei Shizuka was also straightforward about his opposition to Koizumi, calling himself a "dyed-in-the-wool force of resistance." He declared that he had always been against policies harmful to Japan's economy—not only Koizumi's, but also those proposed by former prime minister Hashimoto. Kamei echoed Nonaka's concern for the fate of the weaker sectors of the economy: "Koizumi's reform plans are being advanced based on the assumption that the Japanese economy will be resuscitated if the weaker companies are weeded out and just the strong ones remain. But in truth this amounts to a process of defoliation" (see Kabashima 2002). But Koizumi believed his plans were necessary to shift Japan in a neoliberalism direction, despite the "pain" he acknowledged this would cause.

In a dialogue between Koizumi and the well-known writer Shiroyama Saburo, the prime minister noted that the opposition and some members of his own ruling coalition opposed his policies. He acknowledged that many of the politicians arrayed against him would be pleased with his fading popularity, and that they were likely to dig in their heels even more. But he remained firmly committed to the course of his structural reforms: "I can't give in to that resistance....I have absolutely no intention of swerving from my course." Koizumi's touchstone was Shiroyama's novel *Danshi no Honkai.* (The cherished goals of men). This book depicts two dedicated politicians of the early Showa era (1926–89)—Prime Minister Hamaguchi Osachi and Finance Minister Inoue Junnosuke—both of whom advanced bold policies to overcome the Showa Depression As a result, assassins attacked both men; Hamaguchi survived being shot, but Inoue was killed (*Chuo Koron* April 2002; Kabashima 2002).

In addition to the antireformers, Koizumi had to deal with institutional contraints, both of the institutional dynamics of the LDP and of the Cabinet Office. LDP legislators who opposed Koizumi's initiatives were initially able to block or dilute them through the party's powerful Policy Affairs Research Council, but since power was more concentrated in the hands of the Prime Minister's Office and the LDP secretary-general (who is appointed by the LDP president), Koizumi's hands were not completely tied.

To achieve his goals, Koizumi used the administrative system that Nakasone and Hashimoto had bequeathed to him in a top-down style. He was able to pursue reform more proactively when his support ratings improved. Koizumi framed his reform program in dramatic sound bites that won popular support, but when it came down to actual reform, he was prepared to compromise so that he could at least partially achieve his reformist goals, a process that Noble (2005) refers to as "stealth populism" and sees as a deliberate strategy in which leaders proclaim their determination to enact bold reform and then signal that they are willing to accept limits and make compromises.

Policy Agendas of Koizumi and His Successors

Comparing Koizumi's first policy speech with those of his immediate successors reveals the shift in emphasis from Koizumi's neoliberalism back toward the "old" LDP ways. Koizumi's successors chose what they considered to be electorally expedient policies and put the brakes on reform. (Table 6.1 compares the themes and concrete pledges in the speeches of the four prime ministers.) While the first policy speeches of all four are short on specifics, their general priorities are clear.

From his first policy speech onward, Koizumi used sound-bite pledges: "Without structural reforms there can be no economic recovery" and "Leave to the private sector what it can do, and leave to the localities what they can do" (Cabinet Office 2001, 1). His speech was peppered with overt and implied neoliberal ideas. He focused on economic reform: the regeneration of the economy; economic and financial structural reform, including disposal of nonperforming loans and limiting the issuance of bonds; and administrative reform. Two years later, Koizumi reiterated this in his four proposed reforms in a general policy speech to the Diet in January 2003 (Cabinet Office 2003) that he saw as the cornerstones of his structural reform: reforms of government expenditure, the financial system, the tax system, and regulations.

TABLE 6.1
Themes and Concrete Proposals in the First Policy Speeches of Prime Ministers Koizumi, Abe, and Fukuda

Koizumi Junichiro May 7, 2001	Abe Shinzo September 29, 2006	Fukuda Yasuo October 1, 2007	Aso Taro September 29, 2008
Aiming for restoration in the new century "Without structural reform there can be no rebirth for Japan." Advance structural reforms, including economic reforms, fiscal reforms, administrative reforms, social reforms, and political reforms.	Creating a beautiful country. Loss of family values and the mutual support of communities. Imbalance between urban and rural areas. Concern over the stratification of society into winners and losers.	Recovering trust in politics and the administration. Integrity of politicians and bureaucrats.	Japan must be strong. Peace and security. Without economic growth there is no fiscal reconstruction.
Economic and fiscal structural reforms. "Without structural reforms there can be no economic recovery." Final disposal of nonperforming loans within the coming two to three years. Limits on shareholdings of banks. Fiscal structural reforms. New government bond issues will be targeted to less than 30 trillion yen in the FY2002 budget.	Fiscal consolidation and administrative reform No fiscal consolidation without growth. Reduce expenditure. Minimize the financial burden on taxpayers. Achieve surplus in the primary balance of the central and local governments in FY2011. Small government through administrative reform. Cut personnel at national administrative agencies by more than 19,000 over the next five years. Sell and reduce government assets (halving the scale of government-held assets by GDP ratio by FY2015). Privatize the postal services from October 2007. Open public services to the private sector. Review tax revenues earmarked for road projects (to shift funds to general revenue while maintaining the current tax rate). Regional autonomy. Reform the tax system.	Prevent administrative waste and inefficiency. Achieve a surplus in the primary balance of the central and local governments in FY2011. Reduce administrative costs. Fundamental reform of the taxation system, including the consumption tax. Child-raising. Rebuild education. Increase classroom hours and enhance textbooks. Moral education. Ultimately, advance devolution.	Measures to revive business activity (near term). Rebuild public finances (mid-term). Achieve surplus in the primary balance of the central and local governments in FY2011. Pursue economic growth through reforms (mid- to long-term). "A comprehensive immediate policy package to ease public anxiety" will give reassurance to many groups and produce economic growth through reforms.
Administrative structural reforms. All that can be accomplished by the private sector should be left in its hands. Greatly reduce government funding.		Advance reform and achieve stable growth. Promote both reform and stable economic growth. Disparities.	Fixed sum tax cut. Fiscal reconstruction.

TABLE 6.1—cont.

Koizumi Junichiro May 7, 2001	Abe Shinzo September 29, 2006	Fukuda Yasuo October 1, 2007	Aso Taro 29, September, 2008
Promote decentralization, including of financial resources. Reorganize postal businesses. Decentralization.		Create a plan for regional revitalization. Establish a regional vitality restoration organization. Decentralization.	Growth through reforms: develop new industries and technologies; reform regulations and the tax system.
Social Structural Reforms. Review the Fundamental Law of Education. Social welfare—pensions, medical care, and nursing—to be based on "a spirit of self-help and self-sufficiency."	Healthy and Safe Society. Reform the social security safety net. Education. Enact a Fundamental Law of Education.		Verify pensions records and punish any misconduct of those involved. Revise plan for the medical care system for the old-old. Food safety. Advance administrative reform, small government (lean yet compassionate, able to meet public expectations).
International relations. Maintain and enhance friendly relations with neighbors. Reform the United Nations.	International relations. Proactive diplomacy based on new thinking. "Japan-U.S. Alliance for Asia and the World." No normalization of relations between Japan and North Korea without resolution of abduction issue. Promote cooperation with the Association of Southeast Asian Nations. Continue to assist the reconstruction of Iraq. Extend the expiration date of the Anti-Terrorism Special Measures Law. Seek permanent membership in the Security Council.	International relations. Continue the Maritime. Self-Defense Force's activities in the Indian Ocean. Efforts to realize the earliest return of all the abductees from North Korea. Pursue UN Security. Council reform and permanent membership on the Security Council. Principle of "self-reliance and mutual cooperation."	International relations. First, strengthen Japan-U.S. alliance. Next, relations with Asian countries. Continue SDF international support activities.
Ceaselessly advance structural reforms, leaving no areas exempt.	Early enactment of a bill on the procedures for amending the Constitution.	Environment. Halving greenhouse gas emissions by 2050. Toward a society of self-reliance and mutual cooperation. Continue to advance reforms.	

Policy Pledges Fulfilled?

Koizumi emphasized five broad areas in need of reform: expenditure; financial reform; privatization; tax reform; and decentralization.

Expenditure

The Koizumi administrations made drastic changes in government expenditure. One major change was to the FILP—a huge, complex program that to its critics epitomized machine politics—and is often referred to as Japan's "second budget." The FILP was funded by postal savings, postal insurance, and public pensions. It channeled investments and loans both directly to specific projects and industries and indirectly through government-affiliated financial organizations. FILP's scope was massive: FILP agencies provided low-interest housing loans and small business loans, often without collateral (see Noble 2005). The construction industry benefited from the wide variety of FILP-financed infrastructural projects; and bureaucrats retiring from connected ministries benefited from being hired by private corporations (known as *amakudari*).

Although the programs were very popular with a variety of constituencies, the return on FILP investments was low, and nonperforming loans and deficits were mounting. By 2000 at least 75 percent of all FILP loans were "bad loans" (see Noble 2005, 11). During the 1990s there was a growing realization that to get the economy back on track, structural reforms, including reform of the FILP, were necessary. The Hashimoto administration began revising and reducing the FILP (via recommendations from *shingikai*), and Koizumi accelerated this process, also by creatively using the *shingikai*. By 2006 the FILP was reduced to less than 40 percent of its peak value in 1996, and its absolute value was more than cut in half between 2001 and 2006 (Ministry of Finance 2006, 10). By FY2006, public works expenditure was 10 percent of general expenditure (Ministry of Finance 2006, 1).

In addition, the administration pledged to limit the issuance of bonds, and in the FY2002 budget, the government achieved its goal of keeping bond issuance under 30 trillion yen (Ministry of Finance 2007, 8).

Reform of the Financial System

The Koizumi administration thought banking reform and the elimination of nonperforming loans were the means to solve the banking crisis and pave the way for economic recovery. During Koizumi's tenure, nonperforming loans were reduced as a ratio of total outstanding loans from 6.3 percent in March 2001 to 2.9 percent in March 2006 (just before Koizumi left office) according to data from the Financial Services Agency (2006). This was achieved through implementing "special inspections"; strengthening the Resolution Collection Corporation (legislation permitted the purchase of nonperforming loans at market price and established a headquarters to promote the purchase of assets); and developing several corporate reconstruction funds (Ministry of Finance 2002).

Privatization

Koizumi was able to accomplish his most renowned reform—privatization of the post office—and was willing to accept compromise to do so (see Cargill and Yoshino 2003). The aim was to improve postal services by making them more competitive and to use more efficiently the massive deposits in the state-run system. Rather than immediate privatization, Japan Post was divided into separate businesses for mail delivery, banking services, and insurance, starting in 2007. A fourth company handles salaries and manages post office property. All four companies were initially under a holding company, with a slow sell-off of shares in the banking and insurance enterprises to be finalized by 2017.

Similarly, in privatizing the roads, Koizumi was prepared to scale back his initial proposals. He initially proposed privatization of the four debt-ridden and money hemorrhaging highway-related public corporations whose debts were estimated at 40 trillion yen in 2007 by the Japan Expressway Holding and Debt Repayment Agency. To get his proposals through, Koizumi had to battle stiff resistance from toll-road corporations, the Land and Transport Ministry, and from the LDP's "road *zoku*." The eventual legislation reorganized the corporations into six new companies and transferred their assets (toll roads and bridges) and their debts to a quasi-public agency (the Japan Expressway Holding and Debt Repayment Agency). The LDP road lobby strongly opposed privatization and insisted that the remaining highway construction program be completed as scheduled. Eventually, a compromise was reached that allowed completion of the unfinished projects—covering a total distance of 1,242 miles. Virtually no progress was made on Koizumi's proposal to redirect the revenue from "road funds" (road tolls, gas taxes, and vehicle-weight taxes) away from road construction, thus making them a symbol of his battle against vested interests.

Reform of the Tax System

The principles of "fairness, neutrality, and simplicity of taxation" were touted as guiding tax reforms. Koizumi's policy speech at the beginning of the 155th Session of the Diet (October 2002) stated that the administration would conduct sweeping tax reform in the next Diet session and initiate tax reductions exceeding one trillion yen. Other prominent proposals included limiting the issuance of bonds, tailoring local taxation toward decentralization by reducing the central government's involvement in local government expenditure, reducing individual income tax, and keeping consumption tax at its present level.

Although individual income tax was lowered overall during Koizumi's administrations, the reforms implemented in 2007 meant that although national taxes were lowered, the *kuminzei* (local tax) was raised (Ministry of Finance 2007, 14), meaning that the combined individual national and local tax burden remained unchanged, but local government revenue increased (and local allocation tax grants fell slightly). Phase II of the reforms (from 2007 to the early 2010s), despite promising a fundamental reform of the entire tax system, was short on specific proposals and appeared to be a continuation of current policies, with the goal of achieving fiscal consolidation.

Fiscal and Administrative Decentralization

Most commentators saw local government finance in postwar Japan as a "sacred cow" that could not be touched. Since both politicians and bureaucrats have vested interests in the local government finance system and had formed a "policy community" to protect their interests, the status quo seemed set in stone. However, Koizumi deemed decentralization— and the accompanying reduction in central government expenditure that local government financial reform would bring—to be essential. Kitamura Wataru, a professor at Osaka City University, argues that Koizumi was able to make headway through the newly strengthened Cabinet Office; through the macro targets set by the CEFP; and because electoral reform left party leaders with the power to allocate political resources (Kitamura 2006, 17). The initial phase of decentralization under the Omnibus Decentralization Act (1999) left some issues unresolved; Koizumi aimed to resolve these with his "trinity of reforms." Those were: (1) reform of local government financing, either eliminating completely or reducing national-to-local government subsidies; (2) transferring tax revenue sources; and (3) reviewing the general revenue transfers. This trinity angered many prefectures and municipalities. As Kitamura points out (2006), some local governments argued that the reforms would be a strain, particularly for the local governments whose finances were in poor shape and were nevertheless being asked to cut costs even further. An additional source of dissatisfaction was that the proposed subsidy-tax revenue-source trade-off did not envision a clean break from national prioritization and control.

The subsidies were mainly reduced, not eliminated, enabling the national government to maintain control. Specifically, the local-allocation tax system was streamlined to reduce, but not eliminate, the role of the Ministry of Internal Affairs and Communication in determining the annual amount of local-allocation taxes. The total amount of the local-allocation tax was also reduced (for the first time in fifty years), as were local government-deficit bonds. (Kitamura 2006, 17). Second, 2.8 trillion yen of subsidies for specific public services were scheduled to be reduced or abolished. Third, some of the national government's tax-levying authority was to be transferred to local governments (Kitamura 2006, 16; Kanai 2007). The Decentralization Reform Promotion Act (2006) aimed to continue the structural reform, in contrast to local governments' demands that any responsibilities or services that devolved to them should be accompanied by fiscal assistance. However, the law is ambiguous, and it is not clear what role the national and local governments will actually take as decentralization progresses. Confrontation seems set to continue with neoliberal structural reformists headed by the CEFP on one side and the six main local-government associations on the other.

Amakudari

Koizumi's reforms have made little difference in other high-profile and much criticized areas, such as *amakudari*, the practice in which retiring bureaucrats "descend from heaven" to take high-level, highly paid positions in governmental organizations, semipublic entities, or firms in areas they regulated. Critics argue that *amakudari* facilitates bid-rigging activities and corruption. Over the long term, *amakudari*, which in its narrow sense means the hiring of bureaucrats by private corporations, has fallen dramatically since its peak in 1985 (Colignon and Usui 2003, 59). Colignon and Usui distinguish between the different retirement paths bureaucrats take: bureaucrats moving into profit-making enterprises ("strict *amakudari*" and subject to legal restrictions); bureaucrats moving into public corporations (*yokosuberi*, or "sideslip"); bureaucrats having successive appointments in the public or private sectors (*wataridori*, or "migratory bird"); or bureaucrats moving into the political world, for example, running for election (*seikai tenshin*).

In its broader sense, however, *amakudari* is increasing. Lower house surveys conducted in 2005 and 2006 (the second was conducted at the request of the DPJ) showed that the number of retired bureaucrats working at affiliated governmental organizations and semipublic entities increased by 5,789 between 2005 and 2006. In 2006, 27,882 former bureaucrats were working at 4,576 public-interest and government-affiliated corporations they once had overseen. These organizations received 98 percent of the expenditure for state projects, without going through the bidding process (*Asahi Shimbun* 2007a).

Reform and Representation after Koizumi

After Koizumi stepped down, the policy profile of the country in some ways reverted to its former classic LDP style. Abe was touted as Koizumi's successor, but he gave mixed messages about reform, and in many ways he set aside Koizumi's economic agenda. At first, it seemed as though Abe was committed to reform: he appointed five policy aides—the maximum allowed—including highly experienced politicians such as Koike Yuriko, the former television anchor and a minister in Koizumi's second cabinet, and Nakayama Kyoko, who had been a special adviser to Koizumi— signaling that he would continue leading from the Cabinet Office. Koizumi, however, had appointed more nonpoliticians than politicians as aides, whereas four of Abe's appointees were politicians. And in his choices of economic ministers, he signaled that his main emphasis was on growth, not reform. Abe's rhetoric was somewhat proreform, but he did not actively promote reform, and in readmitting to the party the postal rebels who had become symbols of the antireform movement, he was signaling a swing back to LDP politics as usual. Similarly, Abe initially advocated converting road-tax revenue earmarked for road construction into general-purpose funds (an issue that had been left pending by the Koizumi cabinet), but this was not followed through. One specific difference was that Abe implied that the consumption tax would need to be raised (Ministry of Finance 2007, 22), but he left office without making any progress on this issue.

In his first policy speech in September 2006, some of Abe's policy proposals were similar to Koizumi's, but Abe focused on constructing an open economy; fiscal consolidation and administrative reform; creating a healthy and safe society; education; and international relations (proactive diplomacy). Economically, Abe was less radical than Koizumi: Koizumi stressed reform as a precursor to growth, whereas Abe stressed dealing with economic disparities and voiced concern about social stratification. (Critics argued that structural reforms produced the growing income gap.) He also spoke about educational reform and diplomacy and creating a beautiful country (Cabinet Office 2006), themes that he discussed in his book, *Utsukushii Kuni e* (Toward a Beautiful Country) (2006). Abe described his ideology as "open conservatism," which he claimed was not an ideology but a perspective of thinking about Japan and the Japanese. The "open" was presumably to counter claims that his nationalism was exclusionist and to distance himself from the deterioration in relations with Asian countries created by Koizumi's "fighting diplomacy." Abe's hard-line stance on North Korea's abduction of Japanese nationals (see chapter 5), together with his attitude toward China, helped to consolidate his reputation as a hawk, endearing him to the right wing. For example, he led a Diet group that denies that force was used in recruiting "comfort women" and made various public statements on this issue.[6]

By this point, the numerous vocal Diet members from the countryside had applied pressure; they thought that cuts in public works programs had adversely affected their constituencies. Given the LDP's sagging support ratings, and some journalists stressing the negative impact of the reforms, administrations after Koizumi took heed of the demands of these Diet members; the LDP presumably believed that insufficient measures to prevent disparities were losing the party votes. But these proposals were only popular with some segments of the population, and bowing to the rural districts that exert disproportionate influence over policymaking made the LDP become less responsive to the median voter.

Abe did not introduce a wide-ranging program of neoliberal economic reforms, but the reforms enacted during the Koizumi administrations were not reversed. Reductions in the FILP that had begun under Hashimoto and that Koizumi had accelerated continued after Koizumi stepped

---

6. Some conservatives opposed Abe's free-market rhetoric but approved of his nationalism. This juxtaposition prompted a stream of newspaper articles, magazine articles, and opinion pieces that discussed what Abe meant by conservatism, and what conservatism means (see Takenaka 2007).

down: the FY2007 year-on-year reduction was 5.6 percent (Ministry of Finance 2006).[7] Similarly, the limiting of bond issues, an area in which Koizumi had achieved his goals, continued during Abe's administration, and by 2007, this figure was 25 billion yen, or 30.7 percent of revenue (Ministry of Finance 2007, 8).

Although the public had initially supported the Abe cabinet, the administration soon began to appear ineffectual and unresponsive. It ignored what the public wanted, didn't tackle the issues that people cared about, and instead concentrated on policies that lacked salience—most people didn't care about the conservative change that Abe supported. It was not simply that Abe was unpopular and therefore lacked the political clout to be able to pass legislation. Abe's popularity rose after a fence-mending visit to China and a cabinet reshuffle in August 2007, but he lost popularity because of the type of policies the cabinet pushed. The Abe administration chose to readmit the postal rebels to the LDP, in what was widely seen as a complete rejection of public opinion. Koizumi had won a majority in the 2005 election precisely on the basis of denying the rebels' candidacy and rejecting their antireformist position.

The administration also focused on constitutional reform (the desire to amend the "peace clause" of the constitution); foreign policy (particularly the North Korean kidnapping issue); and making the education system more patriotic. But it often seemed that they had incredibly poor judgment in ignoring issues that people did care about, such as the scandal of the lost pensions and the money scandals involving ministers. Agriculture Minister Matsuoka Toshikatsu was dogged by allegations of bid-rigging in road construction projects and charges that he had hugely padded his office expenses. Tokyo prosecutors were investigating companies that built forestry roads administered by Matsuoka's agriculture ministry and had arrested construction industry executives and consultants. Media reports claimed that Matsuoka had received political donations from some of the companies being investigated. He had earlier claimed that a 5 million yen (approximately $42,000) for a utilities bill in 2005 for his small Tokyo office had been spent on purified water and was then ridiculed by journalists who demanded to taste the expensive water. He also claimed more than 10 million yen ($1.2 million) for fewer than five years of "office costs," even

7. Abe appointed Shiozaki Yasuhisa as chief cabinet secretary and Ota Hiroko as minister of state for economic and fiscal policy—both were experienced with economic policy. But as Richard Katz pointed out at the time, "If Mr. Abe is not personally engaged they will lack sufficient clout" (Katz 2007).

though his Diet office was rent free (*New York Times* 2007).[8] Abe stood by Matsuoka, despite the public outcry over the minister's behavior, which caused his public approval to sink further. Matsuoka killed himself just hours before he was to face questioning in the Diet about the accusations. Abe then appointed Akagi Norihiko, who lasted less than two months as he became embroiled in a scandal over hugely padded office expenses: He registered his main office in his parents' home, only to have his father deny publicly that there was ever an office there. He refused to show the receipts. And then turned up at a press conference with large adhesive plasters on his face, which he at first avoided explaining and then later implied were covering up a "rash." (see *Asahi Shimbun* 2007b).

Although Abe clung to the leadership position despite the upper house loss, he finally resigned in September 2007, citing ill health. As we discussed in chapter 4, the leadership position fell to the somewhat reluctant Fukuda Yasuo, who told journalists that he had "drawn the short straw." Like Abe and Koizumi before him, Fukuda had "inherited" his seat from his father. After graduating from Waseda University, Fukuda worked in the oil industry for Maruzen Petroleum, the company that became Cosmo Oil, and then he became his father's secretary. When his father retired in 1990, Fukuda ran for office in the same Gunma district. He won more votes than either Nakasone or Obuchi, both of whom were running in the same multimember district (see Kabashima and Okawa 2008). Both Mori and Koizumi later appointed him chief cabinet secretary in their administrations, and he was an integral part of Koizumi's structural reform program. But after he resigned in 2004 for nonpayment of pension contributions, he took no positions of responsibility in the party or government.

In the fall of 2007, things looked bleak for the LDP. The party was thrashed in the July 2007 House of Councillors election, and it looked set in its unpopular ways, with pundits blaming money politics and the scandal of the lost pensions. Others pointed to the cabinet's lack of commitment to structural reform (Takenake 2008a), while still others pointed to the widening regional disparities (*kakusa*) that antireformists argued were by-products of structural reform.

From Fukuda's first policy speech, it was clear that his plan was to steer the LDP away from reform. The speech had some neoliberal elements,

---

8. Vice Farm Minister Yamamoto Taku later "joked" that Matsuoka had spent the money on geisha, but he retracted his comment when criticized.

such as references to reform of the social security system based on self-reliance, integrated reform of expenditures and revenues, and cutting administrative waste. But like Abe, Fukuda had a vision of reform that focused on economic growth and narrowing the urban-rural divide, limiting income inequality among the regions.

Fukuda made very few changes to Abe's cabinet; both were old-style LDP cabinets with the heads of six of the factions in either the cabinet or the four top party posts. People had been impressed with the high caliber of ministers in Abe's reshuffled cabinet, who, although they were old-style politicians, were also experienced and moderate. But the cabinet's popularity under Fukuda slid, perhaps due to squandered expectations. Fukuda went further than Abe and actually promoted some of the postal rebels to important party positions, ignoring public support for Koizumi, who had expelled the rebels and built his election campaign on rejecting their beliefs.

Fukuda's cabinet curtailed some of the neoliberal agenda: planned increased medical-care charges for senior citizens were put on hold, as was the plan to convert road revenues into general-purpose funds, that is, until it became the topic of a political showdown (*Nihon Keizai Shimbun,* October 22, 2007). The pension issue continued to nag, and the introduction of a new and very unpopular health insurance system for senior citizens age seventy-five and older was a further blow to the cabinet's support. In some areas, the Fukuda administration's policies ran contrary to reformers' hopes. For example, policies to foster large-scale farming and improve the efficiency of Japanese agriculture were scaled back, and doctors enjoyed an across-the-board pay raise. Problems of politics and money and arguments over whether the Maritime Self-Defense Force should continue to refuel naval vessels conducting antiterrorism operations in the Indian Ocean rumbled on. Meanwhile, controversial discussions about a possible hike in the consumption tax began in the government's CEFP and a panel within the LDP.

When the Fukuda cabinet's honeymoon of support ended, the prime minister's approval ratings plunged and the LDP again looked doomed. Fukuda had to contend with a divided government, and the partisan stand-off between the two houses of the National Diet brought policymaking to a standstill. The administration chose not to use its override to push through legislation. (If the upper house rejects a bill, so long as it passes the lower louse with a two-thirds majority, it will become law.) Although the administration would have been criticized if it had done so, it would have avoided the humiliation of a political standstill. Using the public as leverage might have been a plausible strategy, but the administration did not try this. The administration was unable to maintain a high approval rating or get public support for policies to overcome DPJ resistance (Takenaka 2008b). Indeed, the public had difficulty in seeing what Fukuda's agenda actually was.

Citizens who hoped for reform were disappointed with the lack of progress. The extension of the provisional gasoline tax, whose proceeds are earmarked for road construction and repairs, was emblematic of this reluctant attitude toward reform. Classic approval-enhancing techniques, such as Fukuda hosting the G8 summit in Hokkaido in July and reshuffling his cabinet in August did little for his support, as he did not select any reformers for key cabinet or LDP executive posts.

Adding to the LDP's reputation for remoteness and entanglement in scandal, and further depressing Fukuda's sagging support rates, Agriculture minister Ota Seiichi provoked a public outcry by saying Japanese consumers are *yakamashii* ("nagging" or "fussy") about food safety. He, too, was then embroiled in yet another scandal over alleged padded office expenses, reminiscent of the allegations against former agriculture ministers Toshikatsu Matsuoka and Norihiko Akagi.

When Prime Minister Fukuda saw Komeito, the LDP's coalition partner, make a series of moves away from his administration's policy positions, he presumably foresaw even greater difficulty in achieving his policy goals, particularly with the DPJ in control of the House of Councillors. Most important, he had lost public support and the DPJ was increasingly compelling and persistent in calling for a House of Representatives election.

Fukuda Yasuo resigned suddenly on September 1, 2008, ostensibly due to his inability to make headway with legislation. Most journalists derided his surprise resignation as irresponsible, following so closely on the heels of Abe's resignation. But as Takenaka Harukata (2008a) points out, these successive resignations are connected to the structure of Japan's political system, that is, they are caused by the gap between what the average voter wants and the internal composition of the ruling Liberal Democratic Party that is weighted toward rural politicians. The current electoral system makes it more important than ever for Japan's prime ministers to muster broad public support, rather than to appeal to a limited support base.

The LDP elected Aso Taro their president on September 22, 2008, and he was confirmed as prime minister two days later. Aso contrasted with the more nondescript Fukuda. He was known as a pugilist, a brash straight-talker continually in trouble for his tactless off-the-cuff remarks.

His populist image, easy smile, and passion for manga do not fit well with his elite political lineage,[9] nor does his habit of dining almost nightly in expensive bars and restaurants. He also has a reputation as a right-leaning hawk.

The cabinet secretary normally announces new cabinets, but Aso Taro chose to make the announcement himself at a press conference. Many journalists criticized his choices as cronyism and labeled his cabinet a "cabinet of friends." Reformers from previous cabinets were absent, immediately suggesting that structural reform was a thing of the past. A *Nikkei* editorial presciently commented at the time: "These political reward appointments could raise suspicions among voters that Aso has no intention to end politics as usual" (*Nikkei Weekly* 2008a).

This was an accurate reading of the appointments, as it turned out. Aso came to power as the global financial crisis took hold, by which time some opinion polls suggested that the public was ambivalent on reform: some people wanted fiscal stimulus measures and others wanted further structural reforms (Takenaka 2008a). Aso opted for the former; he put on hold a reform agenda, stressing instead reviving business activity and rebuilding public finances. In his first policy speech, he talked about achieving growth through a package to "reassure" sectors and individuals hit by the economic downturn. Although he mentioned fiscal reconstruction as one means to stimulate the economy, he was explicit that economic growth should come first (see table 6.1).

The Aso cabinet, faced with declining popularity among both the public and their own party members, and faced with the global economic turmoil, chose to return to old-style LDP policies and to attempt to spend their way back to economic health. Some of changes were made following intense lobbying from LDP Diet members concerned about their electoral fortunes. Particularly during the economic downturn, the old guard feared reform initiatives and an austerity budget, believing that they would lead to electoral defeat. The government created massive stimulus packages, and their budgets were a sharp departure from the austerity that previous administrations had aimed toward. In December 2008, the Aso cabinet

9. He is a great-great-grandson of Okubo Toshimichi, and his father-in-law is former prime minister Suzuki Zenko. His father was the chairman of the Aso Cement Company and a close associate of former prime minister and construction king Tanaka Kakuei; his mother was former prime minister Yoshida Shigeru's daughter. Aso Cement's use of prisoner-of-war labor caused controversy for Aso, who brushed off criticism as events from before his time.

approved the largest amount ever for an initially planned budget,[10] and, as well, they decided to sell 31.3 percent more new government bonds than the fiscal year's original plan (Koizumi and Abe had both strictly limited bond issuance).[11] The second stimulus package included cash handouts to residents that critics called a blatant vote-buying attempt. Aso himself confused the whole issue by declaring that he would accept his portion of the controversial 2 trillion yen cash handout, contradicting his previous position that he would not take the money and that rich people who accepted it were "mean-spirited" (Ito 2009).

The Aso Administration's economic policy guidelines (the annual *hone-buto no hoshin* guidelines) were a clear repudiation of the fiscal discipline that the Koizumi reforms had pushed. The administration abandoned previous administrations' pledges to limit increases in social security and increased its budget-request ceilings from those adopted for the previous fiscal year, which were framed under the fiscal reform principles that had guided that year's budget (*Asahi Shimbun* 2009b; Inakgaki 2009).

Aso proposed other old-style LDP programs such as creating a fund for special spending worth 10 trillion yen ($107.5 billion) beside the fiscal 2009 budget ceiling, calling for a review of the postal privatization process, and seeking to mix funds earmarked for road projects into general revenues (see *Nikkei Weekly* 2008b).[12]

As the Aso administration's support fell, dissatisfaction in the ranks of Diet members rose. LDP Diet members have vociferously criticized the policy decisions of their own party in the past, but the party has generally managed to patch things up and pull through. But in the past, the LDP had not alienated important segments of its support base.

10. A 88.548 trillion yen budget for the following fiscal year (*Nikkei.com* 2008).

11. An issuance of 33.294 trillion yen instead of the 25.358 trillion yen originally planned (*Nikkei.com* 2008).

12. The Koizumi and Abe administrations took no action on this, and it was left to Fukuda, who attempted to curb spending on roads and declared that the government would reallocate tax income earmarked for road spending to general use. The road construction and repair works were obviously popular among special interest groups, and this reform would be unpopular among them since projects would no longer be financed automatically. However, Aso planned to backtrack on this reform, declaring that 1 trillion yen of the income earmarked for road spending would be given to local governments. Initially, Aso planned that the funds would be given as a local allocation tax to be used for any purpose at the discretion of local governments. Later it would be recommended that the funds be spent on roads (*Nikkei Weekly* 2008b).

After Koizumi stepped down, rural LDP politicians were able to reassert themselves and their policy preferences. Koizumi had been a social and economic conservative, willing to lead from the top. Abe had been touted as Koizumi's successor, but he was a nationalist, a social conservative, and a less-radical fiscal conservative who lacked the public support needed to push through his preferences. Fukuda, on the other hand, was less nationalistic than Abe and slightly more in favor of economic reform, but he lacked a broad reform agenda. Aso turned his back on structural reform, stating that "although structural reforms…have produced certain results, excessive market fundamentalism has enlarged disparities in income and among regions, placing a strain on weaker individuals and creating burnt out regions. Reflecting humbly on this situation, I will break from excessive market fundamentalism" (Cabinet Office 2009).

For years, observers had been predicting that the LDP would be defeated, but the party astutely and repeatedly managed to regain its popularity. To do so, the LDP made various compromises and changes, such as accepting various coalition partners and a popular leader whose policies the old guard of the party loathed. By the 2009 election, against a background of a sluggish domestic economy and a worldwide financial crisis, the LDP had alienated a large proportion of its support base. It had turned its back on the image and policies that had provided it with a recent electoral victory and faced an organized opposition.

7

Voters and the Democratic Party of Japan

Over the years, the opposition parties failed to convince voters that they could provide a credible alternative to the LDP. Despite occasional electoral success, the JSP was no match for the LDP and virtually collapsed during the early 1990s. The new parties that looked so promising in the early 1990s similarly came to nothing. The opposition repeatedly made tactical errors, and, to be fair, the electoral system helped marginalize small parties. The LDP's control over the purse strings marginalized other parties still further, since they had limited access to the spoils of office to distribute to supporters.

Despite the long-term voter realignment and structural change that we described earlier and the changes prompted by electoral reform, the LDP managed to fend off all comers for control of the more powerful lower house for several election cycles after reform. During the early 1990s, however, voters began to view the Democratic Party of Japan (DPJ) as a contender for power. With two viable candidates per district, competitiveness increased at the district level. After gradually increasing its vote share, albeit with a temporary downturn during the Koizumi era, the DPJ then won a majority in the upper house in 2007 and in the lower house in 2009. Did a stronger DPJ produce changes in the relations between citizens and parties, making politics more accountable and responsive to a broad majority of the electorate? To answer this question we look at the DPJ, examining who they are, what they stand for, and who votes for their candidates. We show that to win elections, the DPJ became increasingly similar to the LDP, and in doing so it actually offered voters limited choice. In 2009, in a bid to distinguish itself from the LDP, the DPJ managed to attract voters with its message that it was the party of change.

The Formation of the DPJ

The Democratic Party grew from small beginnings and was formed in 1996 by a small group of Sakigake politicians and some of the moderate SDPJ politicians. After the New Frontier Party collapsed in 1997, smaller splinter parties formed and then merged with the DPJ. In March 1998, the DPJ relaunched itself when four smaller opposition parties united.[1] In the beginning, the party was jointly led by brothers Hatoyama Yukio and Hatoyama Kunio, who had left the LDP to join the New Frontier Party (NFP, or Shinshinto) and then set up the DPJ when the NFP collapsed. The brothers were both highly experienced fourth-generation politicians and grandsons of former prime minister Hatoyama Ichiro, who had been purged immediately after the war but was allowed back in to public life in the "depurge." Hatoyama Ichiro and his fellow hawks criticized Yoshida's incremental remilitarization as inadequate and wanted to go even further and revise the constitution to allow re-militarization. They even advocated restoring some of the emperor's powers. Hatoyama Yukio was the eldest son of Hatoyama Yasuko, a daughter and heir of Ishibashi Shojiro, the founder of Bridgestone Corporation, and Hatoyama Iichiro, a former cabinet minister and the son of former prime minister Hatoyama Ichiro. Hatoyama Yukio did not, however, intend to become a politician. Instead he earned his doctorate from Stanford University and became a professor. He eventually ran for the lower house in 1986 as an LDP candidate, but then left the LDP and became instrumental in forming Sakigake. He was appointed chief cabinet secretary in the non-LDP coalition under Hosokawa Morihiro (1993–94), and in 1996 announced that he would leave Sakigake to form the DPJ.

In the late 1990s, the DPJ was mainly composed of left-of-center and reformist politicians, as it provided a home for dissatisfied ex-Socialist and

1. These were the former Democratic Party of Japan (Minshuto); the Good Governance Party (Minseito), a union of small reformist groups that had emerged from the collapse of the NFP; the New Fraternity Party (Shinto-Yuai), mostly consisting of former DSP, left-of-center Diet members; and the Democratic Reform Party (Minshu-Kaikaku-Rengo), proreform social democrats.

ex-Sakigake members. For the first few years, Kan Naoto (as party president from 1997 to 1999, and then again from 2002 to 2004), Hata Tsutomu, and Hatoyama Yukio were the top leaders of the party. (Hatoyama Kunio rejoined the LDP in 1999.)[2] These three politicians have all enjoyed colorful and varied careers: Hata was a lieutenant in the Tanaka faction during the 1980s, and then he engaged in the party hopping that was common during the mid-1990s. As we discussed in chapter 3, Hata and his faction left the LDP in 1993 to found the Japan Renewal Party (JRP) with Ozawa Ichiro. When the JRP joined the Hosokawa coalition government, Hata became foreign minister. In December 1994, several of the new parties merged to become the New Frontier Party, which only managed to last for three years before it split apart. After losing an NFP leadership election to Ozawa, Hata left and formed the Sun Party, which merged with the Good Governance Party and then merged into the DPJ in 1998. Gerald L. Curtis commented semi-ironically that during this time many politicians did not even include their party allegiance on their name cards; since they changed their affiliation so often, they were probably tired of having new cards printed (Curtis, 1999). Hata was prime minister briefly in 1994 after Hosokawa's resignation, but he resigned when the JSP left the coalition (allowing JSP leader Murayama Tomiichi to become prime minister) and later became supreme adviser (*saikokomon*) in the DPJ.

Kan has also had a varied career: he was active in civic movements, and after three failed attempts he was finally elected to the Diet in 1980. He became well known to the public only in 1996 when he was health and welfare minister in the LDP-SDP-Sakigake coalition government. In an unprecedented action, Kan publicized the bureaucrats' inaction in a scandal that involved the Green Cross pharmaceutical company selling HIV-tainted blood products. The public was delighted with his forthright behavior when he took on the bureaucrats, and his popularity soared.

Kan Naoto's superstar status didn't last long: after admitting that he had not paid pension contributions for ten months, he resigned in 1998. The media later revealed that he had an affair with a television newscaster. He made a comeback when Hatoyama Yukio resigned as leader of the party in 2002, and although he no longer enjoys his former status, Kan's incisive

2. In 2007 he achieved infamy as justice minister when he said that "a friend of my friend is an al-Qaida member. He was involved in the bombing attack in Bali, and I was advised not to go near that area." He withdrew these comments after being criticized for giving the impression that he had prior knowledge of the bombing (*Asahi Shimbun* 2007d).

intelligence and concise delivery make him one of the most effective DPJ media performers, even though his nickname "Ira-ira Kan," (meaning "irritable") obviously indicates that some people find him short-tempered.

The Party Grows and Changes

Ozawa merged his Liberal Party (LP) with the DPJ in September 2003, further expanding the party. (We discussed the electoral benefits this gave the DPJ in chapter 3.) After the demise of first the JRP and then the NFP (the NFP had originally looked as if it could mount a credible challenge to the LDP, but after internal disputes and defections it fell apart at the end of 1997), Ozawa and his faction set up the LP at the beginning of 1998.[3]

Ozawa, too, is a formidable politician who "inherited" his father's district in 1969. His father was a minister in various administrations in the 1940s and 1950s. Although he has little ministerial experience, Ozawa Ichiro is an astute political operator. He was an underling of Tanaka Kakuei and was known as Tanaka's favorite (*hizokko*). As such Ozawa raised and distributed the massive amounts of largess that oiled the system. His deal brokering made him one of the behind-the-scenes puppeteers, or "shadow shoguns" as Jacob Schlesinger (1997) labeled both him and kingmaker Kanemaru Shin, who became Ozawa's mentor after Tanaka's demise. He began to move out of the shadows in the early 1990s, after Kanemaru resigned in 1992.[4] The media often describe Ozawa as abrasive and aggressive, and he made bitter enemies because of his role in the LDP's 1993 splintering and the NFP's 1997 dissolution. As an editorial in the journal *Japan Echo* (2006) comments, "those who dislike [Ozawa] see him as being dictatorial and operating with just a small circle of close supporters, but he is certainly not unprincipled." He has often been outspoken on controversial issues and is not afraid to champion unpopular policies. He

3. The Liberal Party joined the LDP in a coalition government in 1999 (under Obuchi Keizo), but the relationship soured after Obuchi invited Komeito into the government the following year, leaving the Liberals as the smallest partner in the coalition. Ozawa pulled out of the coalition after a dispute with Obuchi in April 2000.

4. Kanemaru resigned from the LDP vice presidency, but not from his Diet seat or the leadership of the Takeshita faction, when the *Asahi Shimbun* reported that he had received an undisclosed and illegal 500 million yen donation from delivery company Tokyo Sagawa Kyubin. Public outrage at this and at his association with gangsters forced his eventual resignation from the Diet (Curtis 1999, 86). We discussed the fallout from the ensuing fight over Kanemaru's replacement in chapter 2.

discussed his political ideas in his bestseller *Nihon Kaizo Keikaku* in 1993 (published in English as *Blueprint for a New Japan* the following year), proposing changes that would turn Japan into what he calls a "normal country," that is, enacting constitutional reform that would allow Japan to rearm and participate in UN peacekeeping operations, increasing political control over the bureaucrats, enacting educational reform, and reducing social regulation. Ozawa has always emphasized self-reliance, and although he supports the Japan-U.S. alliance, he supports a greater role for Japan's Self-Defense Forces. In 2009, after his meeting with U.S. Secretary of State Hillary Clinton, Ozawa told reporters that a DPJ government in Japan would seek to build an equal partnership with the United States, with a reduced U.S. military presence and Japan taking greater responsibility for its own defense. In this respect, too, he is a classic LDP-style nationalist-conservative. (Ozawa's comments created an LDP-fueled furor, somewhat incongruously, given that some LDP Diet members share his beliefs and Ozawa has been consistent in expressing them.)

After Kan Naoto and Hatoyama Yukio, the next two DPJ presidents had short-lived tenures: Okada Katsuya was selected in 2004 and led the DPJ's 2004 electoral upswing, but Okada resigned after the DPJ was humiliated the following year in the lower house election. The rebound in support for the LDP during this time was probably due in part to the DPJ's lack of dynamism. Okada seemed lackadaisical after losses in by-elections in April, and he did not really come to grips with confronting Koizumi over the deterioration of relations with Asian countries and his continued visits to Yasukuni Shrine. Then the LDP ran rings around the DPJ over postal privatization: the DPJ failed to submit a counterproposal to Koizumi's postal privatization bills during the Diet session, and later the party reacted slowly to Koizumi's initiatives, only after voters' interest in postal reform became apparent. Not only was the DPJ unable to articulate an alternative message in the 2005 election, but the LDP managed to snatch the DPJ's role as the party of reform and left them looking like an old-style defender of the vested interests of the postal workers.

Maehara Seiji replaced Okada after beating Kan Naoto by two votes in the leadership election in September 2005. Initially, Maehara enjoyed a media honeymoon, and most newspapers agreed that his youth signaled the DPJ's determination to bring about political change. Maehara proved dynamic in savaging the Koizumi administration when he claimed he was in possession of an e-mail that demonstrated that links existed between the LDP and Horie Takafumi, the T-shirt wearing, spiky-haired president of the troubled internet service provider Livedoor. (Horie had been an unsuccessful "assassin" candidate in the 2005 election, but at that point he was under arrest on charges of breaking securities laws.) In the e-mail, Horie asked executives to pay "consulting fees" to the son of the LDP secretary-general, Takebe Tsutomu. When it turned out that the e-mail was fake, Maehara was made to seem ridiculous, and he resigned. His term had not even lasted two years. According to the media, lower house member Nagata Hisayasu gave Maehara the e-mail, but Nagata should not have been considered the most reliable of sources, given that he had already been involved in a series of controversial incidents. The event was another in a series of self-defeating moves in the DPJ's struggle to convince the country that it was a viable opposition capable of governing.

Supporters had hoped that Maehara could bring about an open, modernizing party that was committed to reform, but they were dismayed when party representatives selected Ozawa Ichiro, the consummate backroom dealer, to complete Maehara's unfinished term as leader in April 2007. For his supporters, the steady, experienced Ozawa was a solid choice after the disastrous experiment with the young, unreliable Maehara. And, in any case, the DPJ suffered from a lack of heavyweight alternatives.

In September 2007, the DPJ convention confirmed the unopposed reelection of Ozawa as its president. In a conciliatory move, Ozawa selected Kan as acting president and Hatoyama Yukio as secretary-general. Maehara, on the other hand, became a thorn in Ozawa's side, banding together with other relatively young, reform-minded members of his faction, such as Edano Yukio and Noda Yoshihiko, to criticize Ozawa whenever they got a chance.

What Voters Want, What Voters Get

In systems with strong opposition parties, the public can exert control over the policy agenda through replacing—or threatening to replace—the incumbents with a party whose policies they prefer, and party manifestoes make it possible for voters to predict the course of action of the winners. In short, this is a situation in which elections and the anticipation of elections make parties more responsive to citizens' preferences.

Reformers hoped that changing the electoral system would encourage different relations between citizens and voters and create a new system in which citizens could signal clear policy preferences to parties and parties would be responsive to these signals. But to what extent are these programmatic parties actually emerging in Japan, and is the DPJ really responsive to citizens? We can get a clear picture of the DPJ's ideology and policy platform using surveys of politicians that the Kabashima Research Group conducted in 1998, 2003, and 2005. The latter two are named the Asahi Todai Elite Survey (ATES).[5]

The surveys ask Diet members their opinions on a number of political and economic policy issues and to place themselves ideologically on a scale that ranges from 1, most progressive (*kakushin*), to 10, most conservative (*hoshu*).[6] The distribution curves of the DPJ Diet members' ideological self-placements clearly shows the changing composition of the party, even in the space of seven years: whereas the socialists/progressives were more numerous in 1998, that is no longer the case (see figure 7.1). As can been seen, DPJ Diet members are still a diverse bunch, although their diversity is not nearly as pronounced as it used to be. This lack of cohesion reflects the party's history of absorbing various political forces of diverse stripes. It adds to the difficultly citizens have in forming an image of the party as a whole, rather than as a loose connection of individuals.

We are able to compare the DPJ Diet members' average ideological self-placement with the self-placements of each of the major parties in 1998, 2003, and following the 2005 election (see figure 7.2). The averages fail

5. The Kabashima Research Group at the University of Tokyo's Faculty of Law conducted surveys of politicians in 1998, 2003, and 2005. The 1998 survey was conducted in collaboration with the political news department of the daily newspaper the *Yomiuri Shimbun* in November and December 1998. The response rate was 59 percent (297 members of the House of Representatives and 150 members of the House of Councillors). The Kabashima Research Group conducted the 2003 and 2005 surveys in collaboration with the political news department of the *Asahi Shimbun*. The overall response rate was 82 percent for those who won seats in the lower house election.

6. In Japan, the term "progressive" is generally taken as being the opposite of "conservative" and refers to the forces and policies of left-wingers, socialists, and those of a similar bent. One problem with the term "reformist" (or "progressive") is that it means support for changing/reforming the status quo, but it does not in itself indicate the direction of the desired change. So it is possible for a conservative to be "progressive" as well. Some right-wingers could properly be called reformist, since many Japanese conservatives have campaigned for reform of Japan's postwar system. Both the Nakasone and Koizumi administrations can be described as progressive (*kakushin*) since they were reformist administrations: in deregulating, privatizing, and enacting promarket laws they "reformed" the LDP system. In fact, some of the legislators we surveyed labeled themselves highly progressive, even as they declared their support for strengthening Japan's defense capabilities and revising its pacifist constitution—two major rightist agendas. But the vast majority of the respondents followed the traditional definition of progressive versus conservative.

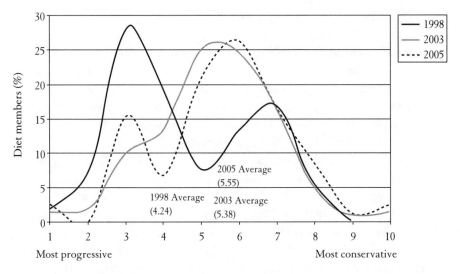

Figure 7.1. DPJ Diet members become more conservative, 1998–2003. *Yomiuri Shimbun* and Kabashima Research Group Ideological Survey of Diet members (1998) and ATES (2003; 2005).

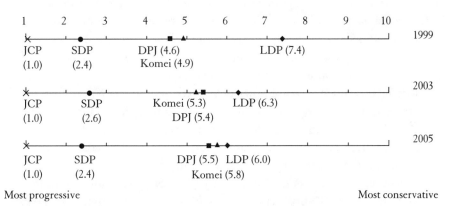

Figure 7.2. Lower house Diet members' ideological self-placements, 1998–2005 (party average). *Yomiuri Shimbun* and Kabashima Research Group (1998); *Asahi Shimbun* and Kabashima Research Group (2003; 2005).

to show the diversity within the parties that is apparent in figure 7.1, but they clearly show the movement of the parties. The DPJ legislators have moved in a more conservative direction, closer to the LDP, while the LDP legislators have moved in a more progressive direction—although they are weighted toward the conservative side. Overall, Komeito politicians position themselves between the DPJ and the LDP, but they have been moving in a slightly more conservative direction (toward the LDP).

The DPJ's shift is electorally expedient, as it is becoming more representative of the position of most voters. DPJ Diet members are behaving rationally by locating themselves in a more central position, that is, closer to the LDP, since the median citizen thinks of herself as neither conservative nor reformist, but as neutral. The ASSK surveys ask citizens, "When you think about national politics, do you consider yourself conservative, progressive, or neutral?" Since the early 1970s, around 40 percent of citizens describe themselves as conservative, whereas less than 20 percent describe themselves as progressive. In 1998 the DPJ was slightly more progressive than the median voter, but by 2005 DPJ legislators were slightly more conservative than the median voter, and they were ideologically closer to the LDP. That is, the parties' shift can be described in classical Downsian terms: the two parties are converging toward the position of the median voter to maximize their vote share—but fear of losing extremist voters should prevent them from becoming identical (Downs 1957, 140).

The increasing conservatism of the DPJ arises both from mergers and from specific recruitment strategies, that is, the removal of Socialist candidates who lost elections and their replacement with conservative candidates, and also by the selection of conservative candidates to fill empty districts. On the first point, although the DPJ started out left of center, in addition to absorbing former DSP members, it also soaked up former LDP members and other conservatives from the NFP (when the NFP collapsed in 1998). It ended up as a welcoming home for conservatives. On the second point, Miura, Lee, and Weiner (2005) detail how the DPJ has become more conservative, not only through mergers and absorptions, but also through specific recruitment patterns.

Miura, Lee, and Weiner (2005) classify DPJ candidates into six groups: ex-Socialists; ex-Sakigake (including JNP nonlabor "progressives"; DSP; "middle" (bureaucrats, business); and ex-LDP (non-Sakigake). Between 1996 and 2000, a large proportion of DPJ candidates were former Socialist Party members and former Sakigake (not ex-LDP Sakigake); the chances of winning were no worse than were the chances of the other conservative candidates (the early years were hard for all of the DPJ candidate types), but when they lost, they were replaced by ex-LDP and "middle" candidates. By 2003 all DPJ candidates had a better chance of winning than they had previously. And it was the conservative candidates who were by then in place to benefit from the increased chances of winning, since they had replaced Socialist losers and filled empty districts, and began to win reliably, as DPJ fortunes improved (Miura, Lee, and Weiner, 2005).

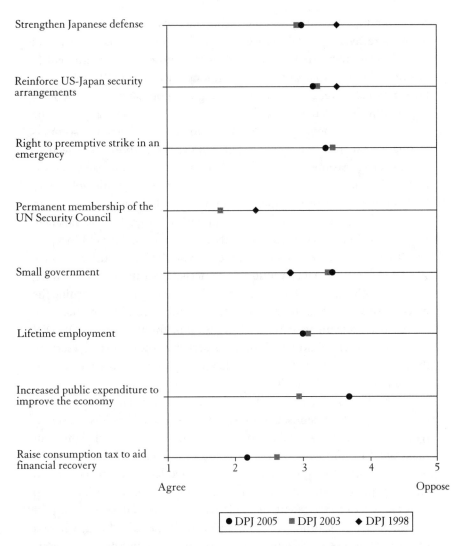

Figure 7.3. DPJ Diet members' policy preferences, 1998–2005. Kabashima Research Group and the *Yomiuri Shimbun* (1998); ATES (2003; 2005).

The DPJ has clearly shifted, not only as to ideology in general, but also on its support for various policies. The party's average position on various policy issues from 1998 to 2005 shows the shift in the policy preferences of DPJ Diet members. (See figure 7.3; not all questions were asked on all three of the surveys.)

On economic issues, the survey asks Diet members whether they support or oppose small government, lifetime employment, fiscal stimuli through public spending, and increasing the consumption tax rate to aid financial recovery. The DPJ movement on the economic system is mixed: By 2005 Diet members were more likely to oppose small government (a position closer to that of the LDP). Among DPJ (and LDP) politicians, favoring small government is an increasingly unpopular position, perhaps highlighting how dependent politicians are on distributing largess. At the same time, Diet members are less likely to support economic stimulus through fiscal spending, possibly reflecting concern about the effectiveness of such measures. DPJ Diet members are slightly more likely to favor lifetime employment in Japanese corporations and considerably more likely to support increasing the consumption tax than they used to be. On security issues, the survey asks about support for strengthening Japanese defense capabilities; Japan-U.S. security arrangements; the right to a preemptive strike; and permanent membership on the UN Security Council. The DPJ is now more interventionist in international affairs in some ways, but not in others. In 1998 Diet members disagreed with strengthening the defense forces; in 2003 they were more likely to agree, but in 2005 they moved back toward their original opposition. In 2005, more DPJ Diet members favored reinforcing U.S.-Japan security arrangements, reserving the right to a preemptive strike, and having Japan hold a permanent seat on the UN Security Council.

Miura, Lee, and Weiner measure party platform largely by analyzing legislative discussions, and they argue that the DPJ is less conservative than the LDP, particularly on social issues such as civil rights, but that the DPJ is more confrontational and more to the left than the LDP on taxation and foreign policy. They examined legislative behavior and analyzed manifestos, and found that the two parties differ most on social issues and, to a lesser extent, on welfare policy. The LDP stresses respect for the state, educational reform, and constitutional reform, whereas the DPJ promotes privacy in information and civil and minority rights (2005, 72). What their data can't show clearly is the DPJ's movement over time.

Analysts often assume that ideology in Japan follows along two axes: the economic system (managed economy vs. neoliberal) and the security system (a hawkish/interventionist role vs. relative isolation). In 2003 the correlations among the survey questions suggest that both the public's and Diet members' preferences on the economy were not constrained by an overall value on the neoliberal vs. managed economy issue; instead, preferences depended on the particular issue at hand: the correlations between the questions on economic issues were low (the correlations between all three, and any two items are low).[7] In contrast, in the correlations between the survey questions on security and foreign policy are high enough to justify creating a single construct to represent a value.

By 2005, however, Diet members and the public understood economic issues in a way that they had not in 2003 (whether temporarily or not remains to be seen). This may be part of Koizumi's legacy—rather than isolated opinions on individual economic issues with little connection to each other, Diet members had started to think of the economic issues as components of a whole system. (The questions were not asked of the public in 2005.)

Commentators often assume that DPJ factions are loosely structured. In fact, although people do shift between factions, or groups as they are called in the DPJ, factions are based mainly on the former party affiliation of the members and as such are ideologically based (see Itagaki 2008). There are eight factions that range in size from Ozawa's Isshinkai (before the 2009 election, Ozawa's group was mainly composed of former LP members), Hata's Seikensenryaku Kenkyukai (former Shinshinto members), and the more centrist Seiken Kotai o Jitsugen Suru Kai (Hatoyama's group of former Sakigake members), to the much smaller Ryounkai (mainly young former Sakigake members and harsh critics of Ozawa) and Kasekai (also critics of Ozawa under Noda Yoshihiko. (This latter group was named after the "Let a Hundred Flowers Blossom and a Hundred Schools of Thought Contend" slogan of the Chinese Communist Party in the 1950s when the party briefly encouraged different points of view and ways of thinking). The more progressive factions are the Kuni no Tachi Kenkyukai (Kan's group) and the Shin Seikyoku Kondan Kai that comprises former JSP members (led by Yokomichi Takahiro, the former JSP member and former governor of Hokkaido who was appointed vice speaker of the House of Representatives). There are also around twenty independent DPJ Diet members who do not belong to a faction.

When the DPJ was in opposition, the DPJ faction leaders obviously could not reward their members with ministerial positions (one of the main functions of LDP factions), but Carmen Schmidt's research (2009) demonstrates that the factional distribution of the shadow cabinet (modeled after the British shadow cabinet but known in Japan as the "next

7. The same questions were asked in a public opinion survey administered by the same research group in 2003.

cabinet") and committee posts were largely distributed in proportion to the size of the factions.

To demonstrate the similarity between the values of the DPJ and those of the LDP in the contemporary system, we constructed two additive scales, one for security/defense-related questions (defense, treaty, preemptive, UN, North Korea) and one (rescaled) for economic-system questions (Keynesianism, lifetime employment, and public works (kokyo jigyo). We rescaled both 0–100, and high values represented economic reform or hawkish values. Figure 7.4 plots these two values and reveals the considerable overlap between the DPJ and the LDP, with the DPJ generally being more dovish and more in favor of neoliberal economic reform than the LDP.

As Miura, Lee, and Weiner (2005) point out, the DPJ agreed with many of Koizumi's key programs such as the privatization of the highways and decentralization of fiscal and tax structures—although on other issues, such as privatization of the post office, the party disagreed with the LDP. In sum, during the Koizumi administrations, the differences between the mainstreams of the two parties were not major policy rifts. The DPJ simply proposed the same plans but with slight amplifications. Any differences were actually relatively minor quibbles about how much of something was desirable.

As we discussed earlier, during the era of machine politics, the LDP co-opted opposition policies when it was absolutely electorally necessary to do so. In some sense, the LDP continued this tradition of "creative conservatism" during Koizumi's reformist era: Koizumi's reforms muscled in on the DPJ's territory as the party of reform. As Koizumi moved the LDP toward the ideological center, the DPJ also moved toward the center, and the parties began to look increasingly alike. After Koizumi, the LDP began to move back toward its former positions and to reject reform, and the DPJ followed suit. Under Ozawa, who is in many ways an old-school LDP politician, the DPJ made a lot of spending promises to the LDP's traditional support base and essentially tried to outbid the LDP, and it is these promises that prompted open and public dissension from Maehara, since paying for the promised programs would be problematic. From around 2006, the DPJ stopped pushing for structural reform and fiscal discipline. Instead, it put on the LDP's classic hat on issues like pork for the rural areas, agricultural protection, supporting entrenched interests in its stance on postal privatization, and it appeared to welcome the LDP's most antireform elements and supporters.

The DPJ attempted to shape itself into a party that could lead the country, but at times, the DPJ's strategy looked more like an opportunistic

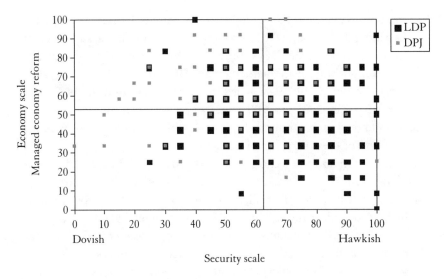

Figure 7.4. Lower house Diet members' opinions, 2005. ATES (2005).

miscellany than a coherent strategy, with the DPJ wearing an awful lot of hats. With the exception of the pension issue, none of the main issues on which the DPJ confronted the Abe and Fukuda administrations was important to the public (i.e., the refueling operations in the Indian Ocean, the extension of the gasoline tax surcharge, and the Bank of Japan governor succession). These were not long-held DPJ policy commitments, and the DPJ was open to the often-lobbed criticism that it was being obstructionist, simply disagreeing for disagreements' sake.

The DPJ under Ozawa, however, emphasized the differences between the DPJ's policies and those of the LDP. Ozawa proposed a series of measures that would increase government spending (including farm subsidies). Instead of projecting itself as a reform-oriented alternative to the LDP, the DPJ chose to position itself closely to the post-Koizumi LDP, making the DPJ look like it was trying to out-LDP the LDP rather than offering an alternative agenda. Co-opting the LDP's classic policies may not be a sound strategy, as it risks raising the ire of the increasingly important urban floating voters, who may view these spending programs as wasteful. On other issues, the DPJ wears Komeito's hat, particularly on social and livelihood issues.

Opinion polls show the public split on the issue of reform, and both parties chose to respond to the antireform segments. The DPJ could have attempted to reframe the issue of reform, not as measures that would cause income disparities, but as an attempt to blunt the effects of the global recession in Japan; but they did not choose this strategy. Professor Take-naka Harukata (2008a), who is strongly in favor of reform, suggests that the main reason for the DPJ's move away from reform was the change in the composition of the parliamentary DPJ after the September 2005 general election. The LDP snatched many of the urban districts. Conse-quently, between 2005 and 2009 the DPJ was a much more rural-based party, and during this time the DPJ changed direction to accord with the preferences of these rural constituents.

The DPJ under Ozawa chose to wear the mantle of the old LDP, prom-ising fiscal support to rural districts and no more neoliberal reform. But at the same time, the DPJ realized old-style politics alone would not be sufficient to pull in the urban vote, and so they embarked on a major media offensive that included the first long-term series of television ad-vertisements run by a Japanese political party. As we mentioned in chap-ter 4, because the DPJ believes that the Japanese media focus on the state, and some research supports this position (Krauss 1996), DPJ politicians believe that they are excluded from this kind of publicity and this forces them to put more stress on political advertisements (Osaka 2007, 24).

As part of the upper house election campaign, Ozawa conducted an actual journey to the countryside and a virtual journey (in political ad-vertisements). On the first point, Ozawa traveled around the provinces for almost three weeks to drum up regional media coverage, and thus win rural votes. According to Osaka, this was a strikingly successful gue-rilla media strategy: of 104 visits, 88 made it into the local newspapers (2007, 26), strengthening the DPJ's image as a party that cares about the rural areas.

Ozawa made speeches in the countryside (on a beer box in front of fields of rice) with tiny audiences, rather than more typical places, such as in front of train stations, which might have led to less coverage and not improved his image as caring for the farmers (see Osaka 2007, 26–28).

On the second point, the DPJ ran a nationwide series of television ad-vertisements for ten months; they ran 3.4 times more advertisements than the LDP. The timing of the DPJ campaign and the single message both worked well (see Osaka 2007, 4). The advertisements were mostly simple, unimaginative messages with a storyline that ran through them. The ad-vertisements' focus was people's daily lives, and the story progressed from "Politics Is Life" to "Restoring People's Lives" to "The Power to Change." In contrast, the LDP's message was scattered and lacked focus. In later DPJ advertisements entitled "People's Voices," ordinary people talked about their anxieties. Without mentioning the LDP, most of the issues the

Figure 7.5. The two faces of Ozawa Ichiro. Used with the permission of the Democratic Party of Japan, copyright 2008.

advertisements focused on were issues that the LDP had not handled well, such as pensions, taxes, and so forth.

The others were an attempted image makeover for Ozawa, the smiling, sometimes even playful protagonist of most of the advertisements, before he later turned into a stern harbinger of change in his final ad as leader.[8] Some analysts even claim that the unified advertising campaign was a major reason for the DPJ's 2007 victory (see Osaka 2007, 4). Osaka (2007) argues that because the advertisements were a success and influenced voting preferences, they marked the transition from old-style organizational politics (*soshiki no seiji*) to the politics of publicity (*kokoku no seiji*).

As an additional part of Ozawa's makeover, the party produced yet more Ozawa posters and leaflets (see figure 7.5). One was a fairly standard poster, except that it came in two versions: in one Ozawa frowns, and in the other he smiles. Hatoyama—with a huge leap in imagination—explained, "We have to tear down the government bureaucracy we have in Japan now. The stern frown expresses that this is the key role of the

8. The advertisements can be viewed on the DPJ's website at http://www.dpj.or.jp/media/cm.html (accessed May 1, 2009).

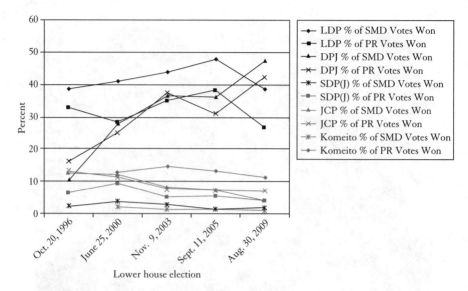

Figure 7.6. Lower house election results, 1996–2009. Figures are percentages of the total vote cast and they are rounded, so they may not add up to 100 percent. 1996–2005 data: Election Department, Local Administration Bureau, Ministry of Internal Affairs and Communications. 2009 SMD data: We thank Maeda Ko for compiling these data from the *Nikkei*. 2009 proportional representation data: Jijitsushin; we thank Okumura Jun for this reference.

DPJ." He added that the frown "symbolizes fundamental reforms to the do-nothing politics of relying on the bureaucracy in Japan." The DPJ, as does the LDP from time to time, finds it convenient to engage in "bureaucrat bashing," although the reality is more complex.

After the upper house election victory in 2007, all eyes were on the DPJ to see what would happen and whether the party could pull off a victory in the following lower house election, building on the gains it had made in the previous ones (excluding the 2005 dip) (see figure 7.6). A few incidents damaged the party's reputation, but they were not the death blow that some commentators predicted, nor was the LDP able to capitalize on the events by increasing its own support. The first problem was immediately after the upper house election victory when Ozawa publicly discussed a grand coalition with the LDP, a coalition that Hatoyama Yukio publically opposed. The general public was nearly split on this proposal, but most DPJ supporters disliked it (*Asahi Shimbun* 2007c). For reformers, the incident demonstrated Ozawa's lack of commitment to real change. Confusion reigned for a time when Ozawa resigned over the incident and DPJ executives successfully pleaded with him continue as leader. Although the party was able to smooth things over, the episode confirmed in some people's minds Ozawa's reputation as devious and secretive. Just over a year later, after persistent rumors that Ozawa's political funds at best lacked transparency, his chief public secretary (a state-funded position) was indicted for allegedly accepting 21 million yen in donations from Nishimatsu Construction Company, a midtier construction firm, in violation of the political funds–control law. The media also widely reported that Aso's minister of economy, trade, and industry, Nikai Toshihiro, also had ties to the company, but unlike in Ozawa's case, details of the investigation were slim and LDP party members did not demand his resignation (*Asahi Shimbun* 2009a).

Despite some eye wiping at a subsequent press conference Ozawa was adamant that he would not resign as DPJ president. He insisted that the Public Prosecutor's Office had behaved inappropriately and that neither he nor his secretary had done anything wrong. (See MSN *Sankei News,* March 24, 2009, for a transcript of the news conference.) The incident was a strong reminder—if one was needed—of Ozawa's background as Tanaka Kakuei's disciple, and it was a serious blow to the DPJ in its struggle to distance itself from the LDP. The broader ramifications of the case are interesting. Nishimatsu allegedly donated the money to maintain "a friendly relationship with President Ozawa's side as he has a big influence in contracts of public works in the Tohoku region," where Ozawa's electoral district is located (*Nikkei.com* 2009a).

Contributing to opposition politicians is not new; even out of power, opposition politicians have some sway, and this is especially true of heavyweights like Ozawa. They can use their contacts in the ministries or smooth the passage of a bill through the committee stage in the Diet. Companies may have chosen to contribute to DPJ politicians as a way of hedging bets on a potential DPJ government. Unsurprisingly, journalists raked Ozawa over the coals, and most editorials demanded his resignation. He toughed it out for a while before finally resigning in mid-May amid public calls from DPJ Diet members. Some DPJ members were worried about an impending election with Ozawa at the helm.

The DPJ selected Hatoyama Yukio as Ozawa's replacement. Some commentators assumed that Hatoyama would be Ozawa's "puppet," a charge that Hatoyama obviously denied.

Hatoyama discussed his own views on politics in two prominent articles, the first, "Harnessing Ozawa's Ferocity," in a newsmagazine in July 2009, and the second, "My Political Philosophy," in the September 2009 issue of the journal *Voice,* then abridged in the *Christian Science Monitor* (August 19, 2009). While short on policy specifics, Hatoyama stressed ending "unrestrained market fundamentalism and financial capitalism [that are] void of morals" and returning to a society of fraternity (*yuai shakai*). His strong support for structural reform during the Koizumi era had by this time turned to hostility.

The DPJ hurriedly made election posters and commercials with Hatoyama as the "face" of the party. Their succinct message for the 2009 election, *seiken kotai* (change of government), adorned their posters along with a determined-looking Hatoyama, symbolizing the party's renewed determination to represent change, a message that resonated with voters (see figure 7.7).[9]

The DPJ publicized a platform that combined huge government spending programs with tax cuts that aimed to stimulate economic growth. The programs were savaged by the media and the LDP as financially unrealistic and in response the party scaled back several of its key programs.[10] In its eventual 2009 manifesto, the party pledged to stop "wasteful" public works projects, promising to cancel a couple of high profile LDP-backed construction projects, cut back on general public works spending, end amakudari, and reduce subsidies to government-affiliated organizations. The DPJ proposed to channel funds directly to families with children, promising a lump sum for each child and then 312,000 yen ($3,460) per annum per child (Minshuto 2009, 5).

In addition, the DPJ's agricultural policy specified direct payments to individual farm households. The party hoped this strategy would win the farm vote, a link that was already weakened by beliefs that LDP reforms hurt rural areas.

During the 2009 lower house election campaign, the parties stressed their policy differences, despite surveys of the candidates conducted by the newspapers that demonstrated some similarities. Calls for structural reform, for example, were largely absent. Instead, DPJ—and LDP—candidates preferred to offer government spending programs that they

9. Their message contrasted with the LDP's "sekinin ryoku" slogan, which sounded awkward in Japanese and literally translates as "responsibility power," and was the LDP's attempt to stress their sense of responsibility as a party and to persuade people that voting for the LDP would demonstrate voters' sense of responsibility.

10. The DPJ's changing policies and spending promises were also parodied in humorous animated cartoons that the LDP produced. In one such cartoon, a young man who resembles Hatoyama Yukio tells his fiancé over dinner all the incredible things he plans to do, and when she asks if they have the money, her fiancée replies that they can think about the details after the wedding (http://www.youtube.com/watch?v=kZpSfahQ--0&feature=channel_page).

Figure 7.7. The lower house election 2009: Hatoyama Yukio and the DPJ effect a change of government. Used with the permission of the Democratic Party of Japan, copyright 2009.

hoped would lead to economic recovery. The DPJ candidates had not moved quite as far from economic reform as had the LDP (*Asahi Shimbun* 2009c), but far fewer DPJ candidates supported increasing the consumption tax (*Mainichi Shimbun* 2009a). The *Mainichi Shimbun* pointed out that, on the basis of its survey of the candidates and despite assumptions that the DPJ was clashing with the LDP-Komeito coalition over policies, the DPJ and Komeito were actually very similar in their policy preferences. The *Mainichi* also found that the LDP candidates were more hawkish and more supportive of prioritizing the Japan-U.S. alliance than were the DPJ, and that more DPJ than LDP candidates supported proposals to restrict politicians' hereditary succession (*Mainichi Shimbun* 2009a).

Throughout the campaign, the DPJ projected a consistent message and image: they were the party of change. Emphasizing this, the DPJ fielded more female candidates and their candidates were younger than the LDP's.[11] After Ozawa's resignation from the leadership position, he toured the nation selecting, and then meticulously training, approximately 100 candidates, even offering funds to some (as his mentor, Tanaka Kakuei, had done before him). The DPJ mirrored Koizumi's 2005 strategy, parachuting candidates, some of whom were women, into districts to run against big-name established male LDP politicians.

The DPJ suffered, and continues to suffer, from a fairly weak support base and negligible local DPJ chapters. In the run-up to the election, however, some of the once solidly LDP industry lobbies began to gravitate toward the DPJ. Farmers' lobbies in only 32 prefectures supported the LDP coalition, as did doctors' groups in only 26 prefectures and construction industry lobbies in only 34 (*Nikkei.com* 2009b). In addition, the DPJ benefited from the JCP's decision to run candidates in only around half of the SMDs and was thus probably able to win many of anti-LDP votes that would have gone to the JCP.

On August 30, 2009, the DPJ pulled off a landslide victory, winning 308 seats (221 SMDs and 87 proportional representation seats). Many of Ozawa's protégés, inevitably dubbed "Ozawa's Children" or "Ozawa's Girls," won seats, strengthening his position in the party (158 of the DPJ's

---

11. Forty-six of the DPJ candidates were female (33 in the SMDs; another 13 women ran in the proportional representation portion only), whereas 27 of the LDP candidates were women (24 in the SMDs and 3 in the proportional representation portion only). (We thank Daniel Markham Smith for providing the breakdowns). The average age of the DPJ candidates was 49, whereas the LDP candidates' average age was almost 56 (Yomiuri Online, August 20, 2009).

politicians were newcomers and 40 of their female candidates won seats).
The LDP's seat share dropped to a mere 119 and many LDP party bigwigs,
including former ministers, lost their seats. Many others lost in the SMD
race and were saved only because they were dual-listed (*Asahi Shimbun*
2009d).

The LDP had not had to contend with such a challenger during its long
dominance. But the LDP destroyed its own reputation for being competent at governing. Its image plunged with the successive resignations of its
prime ministers, repeated scandals involving its government ministers (see
chapter 6), and enactment of unpopular economic stimulus measures.

In opposition, the DPJ had held together and increasingly looked like
a competent alternative to the LDP. During the campaign the DPJ was
a unified, organized challenger with a platform of popular policies. The
party stuck together, limited the damage caused by scandals of its own,
and waited for voter dissatisfaction with the LDP to reach the tipping
point. The voters were convinced: the DPJ had remade itself as the party
of change.

8

AFTERWORD

WHERE TO NOW?

Commentators continue to debate just how much Japanese politics has really changed. We contend that Japanese politics in the twenty-first century is fundamentally different from the politics practiced under the LDP system. A reformed model of governance, a realigned party system, and changing patterns of voter support have altered political life in ways that would have seemed inconceivable during the 1970s and 1980s. Under the old system patron-client relations were the norm, and though citizens did on occasion make their voices heard and force the government to respond to their needs through the threat of electoral sanction, the average citizen was not usually well represented, because politicians only needed to be responsive to a small group of their constituents. However, under the old order, even though they were not well represented by those in power, citizens continued to vote for the LDP, the party that had steered the country to economic growth and brought prosperity and stability at home and abroad. However, when the system's downside—including the immense wastefulness of pork barrel projects and the inherent corruption in the system—was finally exposed by the economic downturn, voters, particularly in the cities, began at last to turn against the LDP style of politics.

The reforms mean that political elites are now more accountable and responsive to voters than ever before and citizens now have the tools to oversee the actions of officials. Increasing numbers of citizens base their party support on their evaluations of parties and their leaders, a trend that was magnified in the 2009 lower house election. To mobilize these citizens, politicians can no longer rely on the old clientelist politics, and this fundamental change, combined with the incentives in the electoral system, is pushing parties toward programmatic issue-based politics that are disseminated through the media.

Voters have become more independent and have easier access to different sources of political information, and they often turn to the media, particularly television, for information. Television now broadcasts more political coverage, and this coverage is more entertaining than ever before. Critics see the growth of the influence of the media in politics as a negative trend that has contributed to the rise of politics as entertainment and the reduction of complex policy issues to media-friendly sound bites. However, we do not see the media as "dumbing down" politics. On the contrary, politicians are now expected to be in touch with average voters, and their actions can be more easily scrutinized—although the media are not always reliable watchdogs. Whatever the flaws of media-based politics, it is obvious that the old-style politics and insider games do not work well on television, either for politicians or party leaders. It is no longer enough for leaders to be simple intraparty operatives: they must now be media figures to bolster their own public support and to maintain their positions as leaders in their parties. Politicians and leaders realize this, but some continue to maintain their old relations and standard operating procedures, since the electoral system provides incentives for doing so, even as they develop new ones.

Koizumi is often given credit for the shift toward a more media-friendly, media-influenced politics, but Koizumi was not the first prime minister to rely on citizens for support or to reach them through the media, or even to enact neoliberal reform. He did, however, take these trends further than his predecessors and was helped in enacting his policy agenda by the reforms to the system of governance that his predecessors had put in place. Koizumi framed his policy agenda to appeal to the public. His reforms became emblematic of broader reform and drew on public concerns: eliminating the privileges of entrenched groups and at the same time improving the economy. But even as he personalized politics, he stressed national-level reform that deemphasized district-level politics, in which representatives relied on providing pork for their constituents, in favor of centrally driven leader-led politics.

To some extent, Koizumi's promises to "smash the LDP" worked. Koizumi destroyed the LDP system because he undermined the faith the party's traditional support base had in the party. The rural areas and organized professional networks no longer solidly back the LDP. Criticism of the LDP exploded in the provinces, and local governments outside the big cities believed that the Koizumi reforms negatively impacted rural areas. Koizumi's successors were unable to spark the public imagination. They were not media savvy, and they failed to deal promptly with issues that the public deemed salient, thus losing support in the urban areas that the LDP under Koizumi had managed to capture. Not understanding the full extent of voter disillusionment, the LDP remade itself in its old image, that is, the as the antireform protector of vested interests, in part because the LDP is weighted toward rural politicians. The U-turn in policies, together with the sudden resignations of Abe and Fukuda, reinforced the image of a directionless party.

The LDP did not fully grasp the reason for its success in the 2005 election: people wanted change. Most people did not understand the details of structural reform, especially with negative aspects of reform being widely touted, but most citizens—particularly in urban areas—want change.

The DPJ under Ozawa—who is in many ways an old-style LDP politician—also turned to the rural areas and started making spending promises. The party won over urban voters as well, partly with promises of benefits. But becoming the LDP to beat the LDP, when the LDP is so unpopular, is not a recipe for success in the medium or long term. It pulled in a short-term vote, but the DPJ government will be hard-pressed to deliver the promised benefits to the rural areas and urban voters when the economy is weak.

Political scientists often look to parties to facilitate democratic governance in which citizens choose between programmatic parties to achieve the public-policy profile they prefer (Stimson, 1999). This has long been a goal of supporters of political reform in Japan. The DPJ finally won control of the government, but, ironically, the two-party system is now characterized by two parties that vie for support by offering citizens various benefits.

A major party realignment is unlikely to be triggered by policy disagreements. Although individual defections are likely, policy-based party splits are unlikely because the classic valence issues cut across party lines. The 1990s were marked by unprecedented fluidity in politicians' party affiliations, but defections have become rarer, and of the handful of politicians who left either party, most did so because they were denied the party nomination. Winning an SMD seat ties the politician to the party (even though the personal vote is still crucial for many candidates, in the 2009 election, established personal support bases did not guarantee success);

candidates run under a party label, in opposition to a rival, which intensi-
fies the importance of party labels and makes switching more problematic (see Reed 2008). In addition, independents rarely win SMD seats. To
some extent, SMD politicians from both parties need their parties to ensure their own survival, but losing control of the lower house—and thus
control of the budget—might prompt LDP politicians to exit the party.
Politicians' party affiliation may be increasingly determined by pragmatic
considerations of wanting to belong to the governing party, rather than by
ideological or policy commitments.

Appendix A

The National Diet

The 1947 Constitution of Japan established a British-style parliamentary system in which the existence of the cabinet is dependent on parliamentary confidence. The parliament—the National Diet—comprises two houses—the House of Representatives (the lower house) and the House of Councillors (the upper house). The Diet is "the highest organ of state power, and shall be the sole law-making organ of the State" (Constitution of Japan, Article 41).

Functions of the Diet: Legislative Proceedings and Submission of Bills

A bill may be submitted to the Diet either by a Diet member or by the cabinet. (The cabinet may submit bills to either house.) Once submitted, bills are referred to the appropriate committee for deliberation. For major legislation, the purpose of the bill is explained to Diet members in a plenary session. The members may then ask questions before the bill is referred to a committee.

A bill that has been passed by one house goes through exactly the same stages of deliberation in the other house. A bill becomes a law after it passes both houses.

However, a bill that the House of Representatives passes but the House of Councillors rejects can still become law if it is passed a second time by the House of Representatives by a majority of two-thirds or more of the

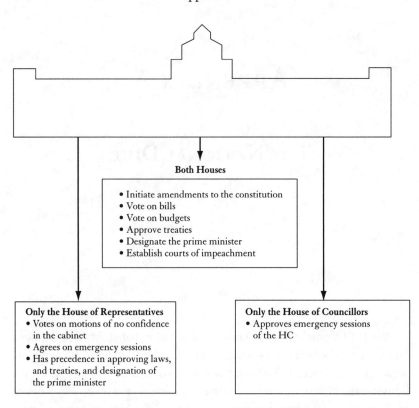

Both Houses

- Initiate amendments to the constitution
- Vote on bills
- Vote on budgets
- Approve treaties
- Designate the prime minister
- Establish courts of impeachment

Only the House of Representatives
- Votes on motions of no confidence in the cabinet
- Agrees on emergency sessions
- Has precedence in approving laws, and treaties, and designation of the prime minister

Only the House of Councillors
- Approves emergency sessions of the HC

members present. (This provision also applies if the House of Councillors fails to take final action within sixty days, not including recess, of receipt of a bill passed by the House of Representatives.) If the houses disagree on the text of a bill, either house may call for a conference committee of both houses. A conference committee is composed of twenty members, each house electing half. (A conference committee quorum is two-thirds of the members from each house, and there must be a majority of two-thirds of the members present for the matter to be approved.) Two chairs—one from each house, with each elected by the committee members from his or her own house—preside over the meetings alternately, lots being drawn to decide who presides first. If no agreement can be reached, the chair of the conference committee of each house reports this fact to his or her house.

Executive Power

Executive power is vested in the cabinet. The prime minister is chosen from among the members of the Diet by a resolution and is appointed by the emperor and must be a civilian. If the two houses disagree and no compromise agreement can be reached by a conference committee, or if the House of Councillors fails to make a choice within ten days (any time in recess is not included) of the date on which the House of Representatives made its choice, the decision of the House of Representatives is that of the Diet.

The prime minister appoints and dismisses the ministers of states as he or she chooses. The prime minister, representing the cabinet, submits bills to the Diet, reports to the Diet on general national affairs and foreign relations, and exercises control and supervision over various administrative branches. The cabinet consists of the prime minister and not more than seventeen ministers of state (including ministers without portfolio and the chief cabinet secretary).

The cabinet has to resign en masse if the post of prime minister becomes vacant or when the first session of the Diet is convoked after a general election the lower house.

Votes of Confidence and No Confidence

If the lower house passes a no-confidence resolution or rejects a confidence resolution, the cabinet must resign, unless the House of Representatives is dissolved within ten days. If a member wishes to initiate a resolution of confidence or no confidence in the cabinet, the draft must be signed by at least fifty supporters.

Election of Members to the Diet

Members of both houses are directly elected by universal adult suffrage (twenty years and older). The number of seats in the House of Representatives was reduced from 500 to 480 in 2000. The electoral system combines a single-member district (SMD) system, from which 300 members are elected, and proportional representation, from which 180 are elected from eleven regional electoral blocs (each bloc returns between 6 and 30 members). Voters cast two ballots: one for an individual candidate in the single-member districts, and the other for a political party or candidate in the proportional representation electoral blocs. Candidates may run simultaneously in the single-member districts and on the proportional representation lists. The winners in the SMDs are then taken off the proportional representation lists and the national winners are determined from the remaining candidates by calculating the proportion of their votes compared to the votes of the winner in their SMD. "Zombie" winners are candidates who lose in the SMDs but are elected from the proportional representation lists (see McKean and Scheiner 2000).

The House of Councillors has 242 seats, with half of its members elected every third year for a six-year term. The House of Councillors cannot be dissolved. Ninety-six of the 242 members are elected by proportional representation from a single nationwide electoral district. The remaining 146 are elected in forty-seven prefectural constituencies, each returning from 2 to 10 members. Voters cast two ballots: one for a political party or candidate in the proportional representation portion and one for an individual candidate in a prefectural constituency.

Appendix B

ASSK Survey Questions
and Coding

The main sources of data are the Akarui Senkyo Suishin Kyokai Shugiin Giin Sosenkyo (Society for the Promotion of Clean Elections House of Representatives Election) studies 1972, 1976, 1979, 1983, 1990, 1993, 1996, and 2003, which were made available through the *Leviathan* data bank, Tokyo.[1] Question and response category wording are exact across years, unless otherwise noted.

Vote

[1990–93]

"In the House of Representatives election, could you please tell me which party the person you voted for belongs to?"

[1996]

"In the election in your electoral district, could you please tell me which party the person you voted for belongs to?"
1. LDP
0. Other

---

1. Gill Steel translated the codebook.

Gender

(Coded by interviewer)
  1. Female
  0. Male

White-Collar Occupation

"What is your occupation? (Even if you're what we call 'housewife' and you help in the family business at home, enter family business.)"
  This variable was recoded into a binary (dummy) variable.

Education

"How long did you go to school? (Leaving a particular school before graduating is counted as graduating.)"

  [1986]

  1. Elementary; current system middle school graduate
  2. Previous system middle school; current system high school
  3. Previous system high school, junior college, university; new system university graduate

  [1996]

  In order to preserve basic comparability, the four-item responses were recoded into similar three-item categories.
  System missing: unclear responses and don't knows

Age

"What is your age?"

  [1986 and 1996] 6-category variable; [2003] 8-category variable

  1. 20–24
  2. 25–29
  3. 30–39
  4. 40–49

5. 50–59
6. 60–100

Community Size

(from sample information)

[1986]

1. Tokyo
2. The other nine large cities
3. Towns with a population greater than 100,000
4. Towns with a population less than or equal to 100,000
5. Villages

[1986]

1. Tokyo
2. The other ten large cities
3. Towns with a population greater than 100,000
4. Towns with a population less than or equal to 100,000
5. Villages

[1983]

2. The other ten large cities; otherwise as 1972–76

[1990]

2. The other eleven large cities; otherwise as 1972–76

[1993–96]

2. The other twelve large cities; otherwise as 1972–76

Length of Residence

"About how many years have you lived in this city (prefecture, town, village)?"

[1986–96]

1. Three years or less
2. More than three years

3. More than ten years
4. More than twenty years (ever since birth)

System missing: unclear responses and don't knows

Issues

Changes in question wording:

[1990–93]: "In the last election, what kinds of issues did you think about when choosing how to vote? If they appear on this list, please say."
[1996]: "In the last election, what kind of issues did you consider? If they are on this list, please say."

Changes in response categories:

[1986]: Environmental pollution
[1990–96]: Environmental pollution; environmental problems
[1972–90]: Prices
[1993–96]: Prices; business
[1990–96]: The education issue
[1983–96]: Taxation (*zeikin mondai*)
[1983–90]: Political ethics (*seiji rinri*)
1. Yes
0. Otherwise

Trade Union Membership

"Are you a member of a trade union?"
1. Member
0. Otherwise

Group Membership

"Are you a member of any of these kinds of groups?"
List includes: Neighborhood groups (Chonaikai, Burakukai, Jijikai)

[1972–90]: Women's Association and Young People's Association
[1993–96]: Women's Association; Koenkai; PTA; religious groups; farmers' unions; neighborhood associations; or leisure groups

1. Member in one or more network
0. Otherwise

Professional: Business, commerce, farming, or fishing association

1. Member in one or more
0. Otherwise

Question from JES 1967

Q28(1-D). "Where would you say the [insert party name] is?"

1. Right
2. Moderate right
3. Center
4. Moderate left
5. Left

Questions from JES I, JES II, and JEDS

Q21."We frequently use the words 'Conservative' or 'Progressive.' Which of the following category best describes you?" (Ideology)

1. Conservative
2. Somewhat conservative
3. Moderate
4. Somewhat progressive
5. Progressive

This question is only used in 1990 and 1993 and is recoded so that the choices are comparable across years. The question for the other years is shown below.

Q21SUP. "When you think about national politics, do you consider yourself conservative, progressive, or neutral?" (Ideology)

1. Conservative
2. Progressive
3. Neutral
Other/don't know

Q50 1–5. "Then what about the following political parties [name parties]? Where would you place the political position of each political party?"

1. Progressive
2. Somewhat progressive
3. Neutral
4. Somewhat conservative
5. Conservative

System missing: don't know, not applicable

APPENDIX C

THE JAPAN ELECTION STUDY II

The Japan Election Study II (JES II) is the most comprehensive panel-survey data available on contemporary Japanese political attitudes and behavior. This survey is a nine-wave nationwide panel survey that began before the 1993 lower house election. Central Research Services collected the data between 1993 and 1996 for the JES II Research Group.[1] Using a two-stage stratified area probability sampling method, the survey targeted 3,000 eligible voters at the time of the first wave. Of the target sample, 75.2 percent (2,255 cases) responded to the first wave of the panel survey conducted in July 1993. As with other panel studies, some respondents did not complete all waves of the survey. Of the 2,255 respondents who participated in the first wave, 589 completed all waves of the survey.

---

1. Members of the research group included Kabashima Ikuo, Miyake Ichiro, Watanuki Joii, Kobayashi Yoshiaki, and Ikeda Ken'ichi. We thank them for allowing us to use this data set.

References

Abe, H., M. Shindo, and S. Kawato (1994). *The Government and Politics of Japan.* Tokyo: University of Tokyo Press.

Abe, S. (2006). Utsukushii Kuni e [Toward a beautiful country: My vision for Japan]. Tokyo: Bungei Shunju.

Administrative Management Bureau, Ministry of Internal Affairs and Communications (2007). *Organization of the Government of Japan 2007.* Tokyo: Ministry of Internal Affairs and Communications.

Akuto, H., M. Toshiharu, H. Mizuno, R. Makita, E. Takagi, and J. Saito (1978). "Gendai daigakusei no seikatsu to iken: Masu media kodo, seiji iken oyobi kachikan wo chushin ni" [Lifestyles and opinions of contemporary university students: Their mass media behavior, political opinions, and values]. *Tokyo Shimbun Kenkyujo Kiyo* [Tokyo Newspaper Research Institute Journal] 26:31–109.

Amyx, J. A. (2004). *Japan's Financial Crisis: Institutional Rigidity and Reluctant Change.* Princeton: Princeton University Press.

Anderson, C. J., and J. Ishii (1997). "The Political Economy of Election Outcomes in Japan." *British Journal of Political Science* 27(4): 619–30.

Asahi News Service (2001). "If LDP Is Intent upon Reform, Election Is the Time to Show It." April 11.

Asahi Shimbun (2007a). "Amakudari bureaucrats increased by 5,789." March 30.

—— (2007b). "Politics and Money Scandals Continue." September 13.

—— (2007c). "Survey: 48% of Voters Oppose Coalition Proposal." November 11.

—— (2007d). "Fukuda Defends Hatoyama's al-Qaida Comment." December 17.

—— (2009a). "Ozawa Out, but Nikai Remains in Cabinet." May 12.

—— (2009b). "End of Era in Fiscal Policy." Editorial. June 24. http://www.asahi.com/english/Herald-asahi/TKY200906250065.html.

—— (2009c). "Calls for Economic Reforms Recede." August 20.

—— (2009d). "Minshu 308 Seiken Kotai." [DPJ 308 government change].
    August 31, evening edition.

Asahi Shimbunsha (2005). *Asahi Gendai Yogo Chiezo* [Asahi Yearbook of
    Contemporary Terminology]. Tokyo: Asahi Shimbunsha.

Asahi Shimbun-Todai Elite Survey (ATES) (2003). Asahi Todai Data Archive.
    http://www.j.u-tokyo.ac.jp/~masaki/ats/atpsdata.html.

—— (2005). Asahi Todai Data Archive. http://www.j.u-tokyo.ac.jp/~masaki/ats/
    atpsdata.html.

Baum, M. A., and S. Kernell (2001). "Economic Class and Popular Support for
    Franklin Roosevelt in War and Peace." *Public Opinion Quarterly* 65:198–229.

BBC News (2000). "Japanese PM Sparks Holy Row." May 16.

Berton, P. (2000). "Japanese Communist Party: The 'Lovable' Party." In *Japan's
    New Party System,* edited by R. J. Hrebenar. Boulder, CO: Westview.

Bevacqua, R. (1997). "Administrative Reform: Searching for the 'Hashimoto
    Vision.'" JPRI Working Paper 36 (August). Japan Policy Research Institute:
    University of San Francisco Center for the Pacific Rim.

Box-Steffensmeier, J. M., and R. M. Smith (1996). "The Dynamics of Aggregate
    Partisanship." *American Political Science Review* 90(3): 567–80.

Brace, P., and B. Hinckley (1992). *Follow the Leader: Opinion Polls and the
    Modern Presidents.* New York: Basic Books.

Brady, H. E., and P. M. Sniderman (1985). "Attitude Attribution: A Group Basis
    for Political Reasoning." *American Political Science Review* 79(4): 1061–78.

Bullock, R. (1997). "*Nokyo:* A Short Cultural History." JPRI Working Paper 41
    (December). Japan Policy Research Institute: University of San Francisco
    Center for the Pacific Rim.

Cabinet Office (2001). "Policy Speech By Prime Minister Junichiro Koizumi to
    the 151st Session of the Diet." May 7. http://www.kantei.go.jp/foreign/koizum
    ispeech/2001/0507policyspeech_e.html (accessed May 1, 2008).

—— (2003). General Policy Speech by Prime Minister Junichiro Koizumi
    to the 156th Session of the Diet. http://www.CabinetOffice.go.jp/jp/
    koizumispeech/2003/01/31sisei.html (accessed August 10, 2009).

—— (2006). Policy Speech by Prime Minister Shinzo Abe to the 165th Session
    of the Diet. September 29. http://www.Cabinet Office.go.jp/jp/abespeech/
    index.html (accessed August 10, 2009).

—— (2009). "Let Us Seriously Consider the Future of Japan." *Aso Cabinet
    E-mail Magazine,* no. 42. August 6. http://www.mmz.kantei.go.jp/foreign/
    m-magazine/backnumber/2009/0806.html (accessed August 10, 2009).

Campbell, A., P. Converse, W. Miller, and D. Stokes (1960). *The American Voter.*
    New York: Wiley.

Campbell, A., G. Gurin, and W. E. Miller (1954). *The Voter Decides.* Evanston, IL:
    Row, Peterson.

Campbell, J. C. (1989). "Democracy and Bureaucracy in Japan." In *Democracy
    in Japan,* edited by T. Ishida and E. Krauss. Pittsburgh: University of
    Pittsburgh Press.

—— (1992). *How Policies Change: The Japanese Government and the Aging
    Society.* Princeton, NJ: Princeton University Press.

—— (1996). "Media and Policy Change in Japan." In *Media and Politics in Japan*, edited by S. J. Pharr and E. S. Krauss, 187–212. Honolulu: University of Hawai'i Press.

Campbell, J. C., and N. Ikegami (2000). "Long-term Care Insurance Comes to Japan." *Health Affairs* 19(3): 26–39.

Campbell, J. C., and E. Scheiner (2008). "Fragmentation and Power: Reconceptualizing Policy Making under Japan's 1955 System." *Japanese Journal of Political Science* 9(1): 89–113.

Cargill, T. F., and N. Yoshino (2003). *Postal Savings and Fiscal Investment in Japan.* Oxford: Oxford University Press.

Carmines, E. G., and J. A. Stimson (1989). *Issue Evolution: Race and the Transformation of American Politics.* Princeton, NJ: Princeton University Press.

Colignon, R. A., and C. Usui (2003). *Amakudari: The Hidden Fabric of Japan's Economy.* Ithaca, NY: Cornell University Press, ILR Press.

Curtis, G. L. (1988). *The Japanese Way of Politics.* New York: Columbia University Press.

—— (1999). *The Logic of Japanese Politics: Leaders, Institutions, and the Limits of Change.* New York: Columbia University Press.

Dabney, D. (2008). "Campaign Behavior: The Limits to Change." In *Democratic Reform in Japan: Assessing the Impact*, edited by S. L. Martin and G. Steel, 39–63. Boulder, CO: Lynne Rienner.

Dalton, R. J., P. A. Beck, and S. C. Flanagan (1984). "Electoral Change in Advanced Industrial Democracies." In *Electoral Change in Advanced Industrial Democracies: Realignment or Dealignment?*, edited by R. J. Dalton, S. C. Flanagan, and P. A. Beck, 3–22. Princeton, NJ, Princeton University Press.

DeVos, George (1984). "Institutions for Social Change in Japan." *Research Papers and Policy Studies* 9, Berkeley: Institute of East Asian Studies, University of California.

Dower, J. W. (1999). *Embracing Defeat: Japan in the Wake of World War II.* New York: W. W. Norton.

Downs, A. (1957). *An Economic Theory of Democracy.* New York: Harper and Row.

Duverger, M. (1959). *Political Parties: Their Organization and Activity in the Modern State.* 2nd ed. London: Methuen.

Estavez-Abe, Margarita (2009). "Voters (Finally) in Command: The Changing Japanese Welfare State Global Asia." *Journal of the East Asia Foundation* 4(1) Spring.

Fackler, M. (2007). "Facing Inquiry, Japanese Official Commits Suicide." *New York Times.* May 28.

Feldman, O. (1993). *Politics and the News Media in Japan.* Ann Arbor: University of Michigan Press.

—— (2002). "Personality and Leadership," *Undercurrents in Japanese Politics, Asia Program Special Report* 101 (February). Woodrow Wilson International Center for Scholars, 30–35.

Financial Services Agency (Japan) (2006). "The Status of Non Performing Loans as of end-March 2006." August 8. http://www.fsa.go.jp/en/regulated/npl/20060808.html (accessed July 1 2007).

Flanagan, S. C. (1984). "Electoral Change in Japan: A Study of Secular Realignment." In *Electoral Change in Advanced Industrial Democracies: Realignment or Dealignment?*, edited by R. J. Dalton, S. C. Flanagan, and P. A. Beck, 159–204. Princeton, NJ: Princeton University Press.

—— (1996). "Media Exposure and the Quality of Political Participation in Japan." In *Media and Politics in Japan,* edited by S. J. Pharr and E. S. Krauss, 277–312. Honolulu: University of Hawai'i Press.

Flanagan, S. C., et al. (1991a). "Media Influences and Voting Behavior." In *The Japanese Voter,* edited by S. C. Flanagan et al., 297–331. New Haven: Yale University Press.

—— (1991b). "Value Cleavages, Contextual Influences, and the Vote," In *The Japanese Voter,* edited by S. C. Flanagan et al., 84–142. New Haven: Yale University Press.

Freeman, L. A. (2000). *Closing the Shop: Information Cartels and Japan's Mass Media.* Princeton, NJ: Princeton University Press.

French, H. W. (2000). "Sympathy for Japan's Leader Ebbs in a String of Gaffes." *New York Times.* May 26.

Gerber, E. R., and J. E. Jackson (1993). "Endogenous Preferences and the Study of Institutions." *American Political Science Review* 87(3): 639–56.

Gibney, F. (2007). Foreword to the new edition, *Yoshida Shigeru: Last Meiji Man,* by Yoshida, S., edited by H. Nara, ix–xiii. Lanham: Rowman and Littlefield.

Groth, D. E. (1996). "Media and Political Protest: The Bullet Train Movements." In *Media and Politics in Japan,* edited by S. J. Pharr and E. S. Krauss, 213–41. Honolulu: University of Hawai'i Press.

Hamilton, J. T. (2004). *All the News That's Fit to Sell: How the Market Transforms Information into News.* Princeton, NJ: Princeton University Press.

Hatoyama, Yukio (2009). Moju Ozawa o Kotsuka [Harnessing Ozawa's Ferocity]. July: 94–104.

Hatoyama, Yukio. "Japan Must Shake off US-Style Globalization." *Christian Science Monitor.* August 19.

Hellwig, T. T. (2001). "Interdependence, Government Constraints, and Economic Voting." *Journal of Politics* 63(4): 1141–62.

Heston, A., R. Summers, and Aten, B. (2006). *Penn World Table* version 6.2. Center for International Comparisons of Production, Income and Prices, University of Pennsylvania. September. Data available from http://pwt.econ.upenn.edu/php_site/pwt_index.php

Hoshi, H., and I. Osaka (2006). *Terebi Seiji* [Television politics]. Tokyo: Asahi Shinbunsha.

House of Representatives (2009). *Guide to the House: Diet Functions.* http://www.shugiin.go.jp/index.nsf/html/index_e_guide.htm (accessed May 10, 2009).

Hrebenar, Ronald J. (2000). *Japan's New Party System,* 3rd ed. Boulder, CO: Westview.

Huber, J. D., and B. G. Powell (1994). "Congruence between Citizens and Policymakers in Two Visions of Liberal Democracy." *World Politics* 46(3): 291–326.

Huntington, S. P., and J. M. Nelson (1976). *No Easy Choice: Political Participation in Developing Countries.* Cambridge: Center for International Affairs, Harvard University Press.

Iijima, I. (2007). *Jitsuroku Koizumi gaiko* [Records of Koizumi diplomacy]. Tokyo: Nihon Keizai Shinbunsha.

Ikeda, K. (2004). "2001-nen Shugi-in Senkyo to Koizumi Koka." [The 2001 House of Councillors election and the Koizumi effect] *Japanese Journal of Electoral Studies* 19:29–50.

Inagaki, N. (2009). "Cabinet Opens Spending Spigots." *Asahi Shimbun.* June 24.

Ishi, H. (1993). *The Japanese Tax System,* 2nd edition. Oxford: Oxford University Press.

Ishida, H. (1993). *Social Mobility in Contemporary Japan: Educational Credentials, Class and the Labour Market in a Cross-National Perspective.* Oxford: Macmillan/St. Antony's College, Oxford.

—— (2006). "The Persistence of Social Inequality in Postwar Japan" *Newsletter of the Institute of Social Science, University of Tokyo* 35(October): 7–11.

Ishizawa, Y. (2002). *Sori daijin to media.* [The prime minister and the media] Tokyo: Bungei Shunju.

Itagaki, E. (2008). *Minshuto habatsu kososhi: Minshuto no yukue.* [A history of the Democratic Party's factional feuding: Locating the Democratic Party]. Tokyo: Kyoeishobo.

Ito, M. (2009). "Aso Decides He Will Take Cash Handout. Now Argues Consumption Needs Boost." *Japan Times.* March 3.

Iyengar, S., and D. R. Kinder. (1987). *News That Matters: Television and American Opinion.* Chicago: University of Chicago Press.

Japan Echo. (2006). "Editorial: The New Leaders of Japan's Top Three Parties." 33(6): 1–3.

Japan International Cooperation Agency (JICA) (2008). "Keys to Japan-Governance (The Structure of Stability and Dynamism)." Audiovisual produced by Nippon Hoso Kyokai (NHK).

Japan Election Survey II (JES II) (1993–96). Conducted by I. Kabashima, J. Watanuki, I. Miyake, Y. Kobayashi, and K. Ikeda. http://www.kh-web.org/research/archive/jes2/ (accessed August 10, 2009).

Johnson, C. (1982). *MITI and the Japanese Miracle: The Growth of Industrial Policy, 1925–1975.* Stanford: Stanford University Press.

—— (1989). "MITI, MPT, and the Telecom Wars: How Japan Makes Policy for High Technology." In *Politics and Productivity: How Japan's Development Strategy Works,* edited by Chalmers Johnson, Laura D'Andrea Tyson, and John Zysman, 177–240. New York: Harper Business.

Kabashima, I. (1984). "Supportive Participation with Economic Growth: The Case of Japan." *World Politics* 36(3): 309–38.

—— (1992). "89-nen San'in sen" [The 1989 House of Councillors election]. *Leviathan* 10(Spring).

—— (1994). "Shinto no tojo to Jiminto itto yui taisei no hokai" [The emergence of the new parties and the collapse of one-party LDP rule]. *Leviathan* 15 (Fall): 9–12.

—— (2000). "The LDP's 'Kingdom of the Regions' and the Revolt of the Cities." *Japan Echo* 27(5): 22–28.

—— (2002). "The Challenge Facing Koizumi." *Japan Echo* 29(3): 6–9.

—— (2004). *Sengo seiji no kiseki: Jiminto shisutemu no keisei to henyo* [The trajectory of postwar politics: The formation and transformation of the LDP system]. Tokyo: Iwanami Shoten.

Kabashima, I., and J. Broadbent (1986). "Referent Pluralism: Mass Media and Politics in Japan." *Journal of Japanese Studies* 12(2): 329–61.

Kabashima, I., and R. Imai (2001). "2000-nen sosenkyo tohyo kodo" [Voting behavior in the 2000 general election]. *Senkyo Kenkyu* 16:5–17.

—— (2008). "The LDP's Defeat in Crucial Single-seat Constituencies of the 2007 Upper House Election." *Social Science Japan Journal* 11(2): 277–93.

Kabashima, I., and Y. Ishio (1998). "The Instability of Party Identification among Eligible Japanese Voters." *Party Politics* 4 (2): 177–201.

Kabashima, I., J. Marshall, T. Uekami, and D. Hyun (2000). "Casual Cynics, or Disillusioned Democrats? Political Alienation in Japan." *Political Psychology* 21(4): 779–804.

Kabashima, I., and C. Okawa (2007). "Abe's Dilemma," *Japan Echo* 34, no. 1 (February): 41–46.

Kabashima, I., and T. Sugawara (2004). "Komei ga dochira o erabu ka de seiken wa kawaru" [Komeito's choice could bring about a change of government] *Chuokoron* 119, no. 1 (January).

—— (2005). "Lessons from the LDP Landslide." *Japan Echo* 32(6): 10–17.

Kabashima Seminar [*zemi*] (1990). *Gendai Nihon no Seijika zo* [Contemporary Politicians]. Tokyo: Bokutakusha.

Kariya, T. (1995). *Taishu kyoiku shakai no yukue* [The future of the mass education society]. Tokyo: Chuo Koron Shinsha.

Katz, R. (1998). *Japan—the System that Soured: The Rise and Fall of the Japanese Economic Miracle.* Armonk, NY: M. E. Sharpe.

—— (2003). *Japanese Phoenix: The Long Road to Economic Revival.* Armonk, NY: M. E. Sharpe.

—— (2007). Op-ed. *Financial Times.* November 21.

Kawabata, E. (2008). "Reforming the Bureaucracy." In *Democratic Reform in Japan,* edited by S. Martin and G. Steel, 101–22. Denver, CO: Lynne Rienner.

Kawachi, T. (2000). "From Obuchi to Mori." *Japan Echo* 27(4). http://www.japanecho.co.jp/sum/2000/270406.html.

Kawashima, K., and T. Yoshiyama (2007). "Victory Bittersweet for Fukuda. Initial Predictions of Landslide Win over Aso Tempered by Reality." *Daily Yomiuri.* September 25.

Kawato, Y., and R. Pekkanen (2008). "Civil Society and Democracy in Japan: The Effects of the NPO Law." In *Reform in Japan: Assessing the Impact,* edited by S. L. Martin and G. Steel, 193–210. Boulder, CO: Lynne Rienner.

Kernell, S. (1997). *Going Public: New Strategies of Presidential Leadership,* 3rd ed. Washington, DC: CQ Press.

King, G, M. Tomz, and J. Wittenberg (2000). "Making the Most of Statistical Analyses: Improving Interpretation and Presentation." *American Journal of Political Science* 44, no. 2 (April): 347–61.

Kikuzo. Asahi full-text online database. http://database.asahi.com (accessed August 25, 2006).

Kim, Y. C. (1981). *Japanese Journalists and Their World.* Charlottesville, VA: University Press of Virginia.

Kitamura W. (2006). "The Foundations of the 'Trinity' of Local Government Finance Reform." Newsletter of the Institute of Social Science, University of Tokyo. *Social Science Japan* 34 (March): 16–18.

Kobayashi, Y. (1991). *Gendai Nihon no senkyo* [Japanese postwar elections]. Tokyo: Tokyo Daigaku Shuppankai.

—— (1997). "Political Participation and the Electoral Process" National Institute for Research Advancement (NIRA Seisaku Kenkyu) 9(12).

Krauss, E. S. (1989). "Politics and the Policymaking Process." In *Democracy in Japan,* edited by T. Ishida and E. S. Krauss, 39–64. Pittsburgh, PA: University of Pittsburgh Press.

—— (1996). "Portraying the State: NHK Television News and Politics." In *Media and Politics in Japan,* edited by S. J. Pharr and E. S. Krauss, 89–129. Honolulu: University of Hawai'i Press.

—— (2000). *Broadcasting Politics in Japan: NHK and Television News.* Ithaca, NY: Cornell University Press.

—— (2002). "The Media's Role in a Changing Japanese Electorate." Washington DC: Woodrow Wilson International Center. Asia Program Special Report (February 2002), 6–12.

Krauss, E. S., and T. Ishida (1989). "Japanese Democracy in Perspective." In *Democracy in Japan,* edited by T. Ishida and E. S. Krauss, 327–39. Pittsburgh: University of Pittsburgh Press.

Krauss, E. S., and B. Nyblade (2004). "'Presidentialization' in Japan? The Prime Minister, Media, and Elections in Japan." *British Journal of Political Science.* 35(2): 357–68.

Krauss, E. S., and R. Pekkanen (2008). "Reforming the Liberal Democratic Party." In *Democratic Reform in Japan: Assessing the Impact,* edited by S. L. Martin and G. Steel, 11–37. Boulder, CO: Lynne Rienner.

Kume, I. (1996). "Cooptation or New Possibility? Japanese Labor Politics in the Era of Neo-Conservatism." In *State and Administration in Japan and Germany: A Comparative Perspective on Continuity and Change,* edited by M. Muramatsu and F. Naschold, 221–45. Berlin: Walter de Gruyter.

Kuznets, S. (1963). "Quantitative Aspects of Economic Growth of Nations: Distribution of Income by Size." *Economic Development and Cultural Change* 1(2): 1–80.

Leighley, J. (1996). "Group Membership and the Mobilization of Political Participation." *Journal of Politics* 58 (May): 447–63.

Lodge, M., M. R. Steenbergen, and S. Brau (1995). "The Responsive Voter: Campaign Information and the Dynamics of Candidate Evaluation." *American Political Science Review* 89(2): 309–26.

Lowi, T. J. (1985) *The "Personal" President: Power Invested, Promise Unfulfilled.* Ithaca, NY: Cornell University Press.

Maejima, S. (2001). "Leadership: The Real Question Facing Next LDP Head." *Asahi Shimbun.* April 19.

Mainichi Daily News (2001). "Cabinet Support Rating." February 9.

Mainichi Shimbun (2009a). "Close-up 2009: shugiinsen: zenyukensha Survey Minshu Komei [Close-up 2009 all candidate survey DPJ Komeito: Surprising proximity]. August 20.

—— (2009b). "Shuinsen: Koizumi Children taijo Shosenkyoku de tsugi Rakusen" [Lower house election: Koizumi children exit one district after another lost]. August 31.

Manin, B. (1997). *The Principles of Representative Government.* Cambridge: Cambridge University Press.

Manin, B., A. Przeworski, and S. C. Stokes (1999). Introduction to *Democracy, Accountability, and Representation,* edited by A. Przeworski, S. C. Stokes, and B. Manin, 1–26. Cambridge: Cambridge University Press.

Maravall, M. M. (2003). "Accountability and Manipulation." In *Democracy, Accountability, and Representation,* edited by A. Przeworski, S. C. Stokes, and B. Manin, 154–96. Cambridge: Cambridge University Press.

Masuyama, M. (2001). "Shusho no Jinin to Shijiritsu" [Prime minister survival and cabinet approval]. *Kokyo Sentaku no Kenkyu* [Public choice studies] 37:14–24.

—— (2007). "The Survival of Prime Ministers and the House of Councillors." *Social Science Japan Journal* 10(1): 81–93.

Masuzoe, Y. (2000). "General Election 2000." *Japan Echo* 27(5). http://www.japanecho.co.jp/sum/2000/270507.html (accessed August 10, 2009).

McKean, M., and E. Scheiner (2000). "Japan's New Electoral System: La plus ça change." *Electoral Studies* 19(4): 447–77.

Ministry of Finance (MoF) (1997). *Financial System Reform: Toward the Early Achievement of Reform.* http://www.fsa.go.jp/p_mof/english/big-bang/ebb32.htm (accessed May 1, 2009).

—— (2002). *Understanding the Japanese Budget.* http://www.mof.go.jp/english/budget/brief/2002/2002-01.htm (accessed June 1, 2005).

—— (2006). *Current Japanese Fiscal Conditions and Issues to be Considered.* http://www.mof.go.jp/english/budget/pamphlet/cjfc2006.pdf (accessed May 1, 2007).

—— (2007). *Current Japanese Fiscal Conditions and Issues to be Considered.* http://www.mof.go.jp/english/budget/pamphlet/cjfc2007.pdf (accessed May 10, 2009).

Ministry of Foreign Affairs (MoFA) (2008). "Abductions of Japanese Citizens by North Korea." http://www.mofa.go.jp/region/asia-paci/n_korea/abduction/index.html (accessed April 18, 2009).

Minshuto (2009). "Manifesto." Democratic Party of Japan. http://www.dpj.or.jp/special/manifesto2009/pdf/manifesto_2009.pdf (accessed August 22, 2009).

Miura, M., K. Y. Lee, R. Weiner (2005). "Who Are the DPJ? Policy Positioning and Recruitment Strategy." *Asian Perspective* 29(1): 49–77.

Miyake, I. (1991). "Types of Partisanship, Partisan Attitudes, and Voting Choices." In *The Japanese Voter*, edited by S. C. Flanagan et al., 226–64. New Haven: Yale University Press.

—— (1992). "89-nen Sangiin Senkyo to 'Seito Saihensei'" [The 89 Upper House Election and Party Re-organization] *Leviathan* 10: 32–61.

MSN Sankei News (2008). "DPJ's Devastation: Maehara's Critique of the Manifesto." June 13.

Mulgan, A. G. (2002). *Japan's Failed Revolution: Koizumi and the Politics of Economic Reform.* Canberra, Australia: Asia Pacific Press.

Murakami, Y. (1984). *Shin chukan taishu no jidai* [The age of the new middle mass]. Tokyo: Chuokoron-Shinsha.

Muramatsu, M. (1987). "In Search of National Identity: The Politics and Policy of the Nakasone Administration." Special edition, *Journal of Japanese Studies* 13(Summer): 307–42.

Muramatsu, M., and E. S. Krauss (1984). "Bureaucrats and Politicians in Policymaking: The Case of Japan." *American Political Science Review* 78(1): 126–46.

Muramatsu, M., and I. Kume (1988). "Recent Administrative Developments in Japan." *Governance* 1(4): 469–78.

Muraoka, Akitoshi (2009). "Political Pulse. Women Hold Key to DPJ Success. Ozawa Figures Female Candidates Will Have Edge over LDP Rivals." *Daily Yomiuri Online.* August 6. http://www.yomiuri.co.jp/dy/columns/commentary/20090807dy01.htm (accessed August 28, 2009).

Nakami, T. (2003). *Shusho hosakan* [Assistants to the prime minister] Tokyo: NHK Press.

Nardulli, P. F. (1995). "The Concept of a Critical Realignment, Electoral Behavior, and Political Change." *American Political Science Review* 89(1): 10–22.

Narita, N., and K. Eda (2002). "How the Prime Minister Is Kept from Leading." *Japan Echo.* June 29.

Newman, B. (2002). "Bill Clinton's Approval Ratings: The More Things Change, the More They Stay the Same." *Political Research Quarterly* 55(4): 781–804.

New York Times (2007). "Facing Inquiry, Japanese Official Commits Suicide." May 28.

Niemi, R. G., and H. F. Weisberg (1984). *Controversies in Voting Behavior.* Washington, DC: CQ Press.

—— (1993). *Classics in Voting Behavior.* Washington, DC: CQ Press.

Nikkei.com (2008). "Cabinet Approves Record Budget." December 24. http://www.nni.nikkei.co.jp/AC/TNKS/Search/Nni20081224D24JF971.htm.

—— (2009a). "Ozawa's Secretary Indicted Over Fundraising Scandal." March 24. http://www.nni.nikkei.co.jp/e/ac/TNKS/Nni20090324D24JF022.htm.

—— (2009b). The Nikkei LDP Losing Grip On Doctors, Other Longtime Allies." August 20, morning edition. http://www.nni.nikkei.co.jp/e/ac/tnks/Nni20090819D19JFF06.htm.

Nikkei Weekly (2008a). Editorial: "Aso's Cabinet Picks Include Too Many Reward Appointments." September 25. http://www.nni.nikkei.co.jp/AC/TNKS/Search/Nni20080925D25HH811.htm.

—— (2008b). "Reform in Reverse Gear." December 08. http://www.nni.nikkei.co.jp/AC/TNW/Search/Nni20081208FP6TOP01.htm.

Nippon Shimbun Kyokai (NSK or Japan Newspaper Publishers and Editors Association) (2008). Annual survey. http://www.pressnet.or.jp/adarc/index.html (accessed August 14, 2009).

Noble, G. W. (2005). "Stealth Populism: Administrative Reform in Japan." Paper presented at the Conference on Repositioning of Public Governance: Global Experience and Challenges, Civil Services Development Institute, National Taiwan University, November 18–19, in Taipei, Taiwan.

Norris, P. (1999). *Critical Citizens: Global Support for Democratic Government.* Oxford: Oxford University Press.

Osaka, I. (2006). "Koizumi Gekijo in terebi 05-nen sosenkyo no telepolitcs "naisen" toshite no kaikaku, sono hyosho to shohi" [Telepolitics in the 2005 general election Koizumi theater: The symbols and consumption of reform as civil war]. Paper presented at the Nihon Seiji Gakkai [Japanese Political Science Association], Sophia University, May 20, Tokyo, Japan.

—— (2007). Ozawa Ichiro no Ryo Minshuto no terebi CM kyanpen. [Ozawa Ichiro's journeys: The TV election campaign of the DPJ]. *Asahi Soken Report* AIR 21, 208 (September), 2–31.

Ostrom, C. W., and D. M. Simon (1985). "Promise and Performance: A Dynamic Model of Presidential Popularity." *American Journal of Political Science* 79(2): 334–58.

—— (1988). "The President's Public." *American Journal of Political Science* 32:1096–1119.

—— (1989). "The Man in the Teflon Suit: The Environmental Connection, Political Drama, and Popular Support in the Reagan Presidency." *Public Opinion Quarterly* 53(3): 353–87.

Otake, H. (1997). *Seikai saihen no kenkyu: Shin senkyo seido ni yoru sosenkyo* [A study of political realignment: The first election under the new electoral system]. Tokyo: Yuhikaku.

—— (1998). Overview of *How Electoral Reform Boomeranged: Continuity in Japanese Campaigning Style,* edited by H. Otake. JCIE Papers 23. Tokyo: Japan Center for International Exchange.

—— (2003). *Nihongata Populism* [Japanese-style populism]. Tokyo: Chuko Koronsha.

Ozawa, I. 1994. *Blueprint for a New Japan* [*Nihon Kaizo Keikaku*], translated by Louisa Rubinfien. Tokyo: Kodansha.

Page, B. I., and R. Y. Shapiro (1992). *The Rational Public.* Chicago: University of Chicago Press.

Pekkanen, R., B. Nyblade, and E. S. Krauss (2006). "Electoral Incentives in Mixed-Member Systems: Party, Posts, and Zombie Politicians in Japan." *American Political Science Review* 100(2): 183–93.

Pempel, T. J. (1974). "The Bureaucratization of Policymaking in Postwar Japan." *American Journal of Political Science* 18 (4): 647–64.

—— (1982). *Policy and Politics in Japan: Creative Conservatism.* Philadelphia: Temple University Press.

—— (1998). *Regime Shift: Comparative Dynamics of the Japanese Political Economy.* Ithaca, NY: Cornell University Press.

—— (1999). "Structural Gaiatsu: International Finance and Political Change in Japan." *Comparative Political Studies* 32(8): 907–32.

Pharr, S. J. (1996). "Media As Trickster in Japan: A Comparative Perspective." In *Media and Politics in Japan,* edited by S. J. Pharr and E. S. Krauss, 19–44. Honolulu: University of Hawai'i Press.

—— (2000). "Officials' Misconduct and Public Distrust: Japan and the Trilateral Democracies." In *Disaffected Democracies: What's Troubling the Trilateral Countries?,* edited by S. J. Pharr and R. D. Putnam, 173–201. Princeton, NJ: Princeton University Press.

Pharr, S. J., and E. S. Krauss, eds. (1996). *Media and Politics in Japan.* Honolulu: University of Hawai'i Press.

Popkin, S. L. (1991). *The Reasoning Voter.* Chicago: University of Chicago Press.

—— (2006). "Changing Media, Changing Politics." *Perspectives on Politics* 4(2): 327–41.

Powell, G. B., and G. Whitten. (1993). "A Cross-National Analysis of Economic Voting: Taking Account of the Political Context." *American Journal of Political Science* 37(2): 391–414.

Ramseyer, J. M., and F. M. Rosenbluth (1993). *Japan's Political Marketplace.* Cambridge, MA: Harvard University Press.

Reed, S. R. (1996). "Bumu no seiji: Shin jiyu kurabu kara Hosokawa renritsu seiken e" [Politics boom: From the New Liberal Club to the Hosokawa coalition government]. *Leviathan* 18: 61–70.

—— (2003). "The Political Context of the 1996 and 2000 Elections." In *Japanese Electoral Politics: Creating a New Party System,* edited by S. R. Reed, 1–6. London: RoutledgeCurzon.

Reed, S. R., and G. G. Brunk (1984). "A Test of Two Theories of Economically Motivated Voting: The Case of Japan." *Comparative Politics* 17(1): 55–66.

Reed, S. R., and M. F. Thies (2001). "The Consequences of Electoral Reform in Japan." In *Mixed-Member Electoral Systems: The Best of Both Worlds?,* edited by M. S. Shugart and M. P. Wattenberg. Oxford: Oxford University Press.

RIALS (2007). "Deterioration or Revitalization: Road to Vitalization of Labor Unions." Report of the Study Committee on Contemporary Issues of Labor Unions, Chairman Keisuke Nakamura, University of Tokyo. Rengo's Research Institute for Advancement of Living Standards (RIALS). http://rengo-soken. or.jp/english/en-report/fy2005/deterioration-or-revitalizatio.html (accessed August 11, 2009).

Richardson, B. M. (1991). "Japanese Voting Behavior in Comparative Perspective." In *The Japanese Voter,* edited by S. C. Flanagan et al., 3–46. New Haven: Yale University Press.

Rosenstone, S. J., and J. M. Hansen (1993). *Mobilization, Participation, and Democracy in America.* New York: Macmillan.

Samuels, R. J. (2001). "Kishi and Corruption: An Anatomy of the 1955 System." JPRI Working Paper 83 (December).

Sankei News (2009). *Ozawashi zoku tokaiken* (1): *Kokumin no gawa ni tatta sikenjitsugen ga watashi no saijo no shigoto.* [Ozawa Interview Series, no. 1: My final work is an administration that stands on the side of the citizen]. March 24. http://sankei.jp.msn.com/politics/situation/090324/stt0903242337009-n1.htm (accessed May 1, 2009).

Sato, S., and T. Matsuzaki (1986). *Jiminto Seiken* [The LDP Government]. Tokyo: Chuo Koron Sha.

Schaller, M. (1995). "America's Favorite War Criminal: Kishi Nobusuke and the Transformation of U.S.-Japan Relations." JPRI Working Paper 11 (July).

Scheiner, E. (2005). *Democracy without Competition in Japan: Opposition Failure in a One-Party Dominant State.* Cambridge: Cambridge University Press.

Schlesinger, J. M. (1997). *Shadow Shogun: The Rise and Fall of Japan's Postwar Political Machine.* New York: Simon and Schuster.

Schmidt, C. (2009). "The DPJ and Their Factions: Ideological Diversification and the Struggle for Posts." Paper presented at the Contemporary Japan Group, Institute of Social Science, University of Tokyo, April 10, Tokyo, Japan.

Schoppa, L. (2006). *Race for the Exits: The Unraveling of Japan's System of Social Protection.* Ithaca, NY: Cornell University Press,

Shimizu, M. (2005). *Kantei shudo: Koizumi Junichiro no kakumei* [Cabinet leadership: Koizumi Junichiro's revolution]. Tokyo: Nihon Keizai Shinbunsha.

Shinoda, T. (2000). *Leading Japan: The Role of the Prime Minister.* Westport, CT: Praeger.

—— (2004). *Kantei shudo* leadership no yukue [Cabinet diplomacy: the direction of political leadership]. Tokyo: Nihon Keizai Shinbunsha.

—— (2006). "Koizumi's Policy Leadership." Vanderbilt University. September 15. http://e-archive.vanderbilt.edu/handle/1803/621?show=full (accessed May 4, 2009).

—— (2007). *Koizumi Diplomacy: Japan's Kantei Approach to Foreign and Defense Affairs.* Seattle: University of Washington Press.

Stimson, J. A. A. (1999). "Party Government and Responsiveness." In *Democracy, Accountability, and Representation,* edited by A. Przeworski, S. C. Stokes, and B. Manin, 197–221. New York: Cambridge University Press.

Stockwin, J. A. A. (1996). *Leaders and Leadership in Japan.* Richmond, Surrey, UK: Japan Library.

—— (1999). *Japan: Divided Politics in a Growth Economy.* New York: W. W. Norton.

Takenaka, H. (2002). "Introducing Junior Ministers and Reforming the Diet in Japan." *Asian Survey* 42(6): 928–39.

—— (2003). "Democratic Deepening in Japan in the 1990s: How Can We Make Sense of a Series of Reforms of Political Institutions in the 1990s?" Paper presented at the Convention on Contemporary Japanese Politics, University of Tokyo, May 3, Tokyo, Japan.

—— (2007). "Fukuda's Rise and the Return to the Old LDP." *Japan Echo* 34(6): 42–47.

—— (2008a). "Déjà Vu: Sudden Prime Ministerial Resignations." *Japan Echo* 35(6). http://www.japanecho.co.jp/sum/2008/350606.html (accessed May 1, 2009).

—— (2008b). "Policy Paralysis." *Japan Echo* 35(3). http://www.japanecho.co.jp/sum/2008/350309.html (accessed December 1, 2008).

Tanaka, A., and S. Martin (2003). "The New Independent Voter and the Evolving Japanese Party System." *Asian Perspective* 27(3): 21–51.

Taniguchi, Masaki (2004). "Changing Media, Changing Politics in Japan." Working paper, 21st Century Centers of Excellence (COE) Program Invention of Policy Systems in Advanced Countries: Building a Synergy Core for Comparative Policy System Studies, University of Tokyo.

—— (2007). "Changing Media, Changing Politics in Japan." *Japanese Journal of Political Science* 8(1): 147–66.

Thayer, N. B. (1969). *How the Conservatives Rule Japan*. Princeton, NJ: Princeton University Press.

Time (1960). "Bonus to Be Wisely Spent." January 25.

Uesugi, T. (2006). *Koizumi no shori, media no haiboku*. [Victory for Koizumi, defeat for the media]. Tokyo: Soshisha.

Verba, S., and N. H. Nie (1972). *Participation in America: Political Democracy and Social Equality*. New York: Harper and Row.

Vogel, S. K. (1996). *Freer Markets, More Rules: Regulatory Reforms in Advanced Industrial Countries*. Ithaca, NY: Cornell University Press.

Watanuki, J. (1991). "Social Structure and Voting Behavior." In *The Japanese Voter*, by S. C. Flanagan et al., 49–83. New Haven: Yale University Press.

Weyland, K. (1999). "Neoliberal Populism in Latin America and Eastern Europe." *Comparative Politics* 34(4): 379–401.

—— (2001). "Clarifying a Contested Concept: Populism in the Study of Latin American Politics." *Comparative Politics* 34(1): 1–21.

Wilson, J. Q. (1973) *Political Organizations*. New York: Basic Books.

Wolferen, K. V. (1989). *The Enigma of Japanese Power: People and Politics in a Stateless Nation*. London: Macmillan.

Yamada, M. (2004). "The Effectiveness of Adopting a Populist Strategy and the Importance of Trust." Paper presented at the Conference of the Nihon Seiji Gakkai [Japanese Political Science Association], October 2, Sapporo University, Hokkaido, Japan.

Yamada, M., G. Steel, K. Inamasu, K. Ikeda, and N. Taniguchi. (2008). "Country Assessment Report on the State of Democratic Governance. Japan: Pessimism in Mature Democracy." Asian Barometer Conference on the State of Democratic Governance in Asia, Session II: Democratic Regimes

in Northeast Asia. www.asianbarometer.org/newenglish/publications/
conferencepapers/2008conference/sec.2.1.pdf.

Yomiuri Online (2009). "Josei ha Sengo saita 17%, Sengo Umare 86%…
kohoshabunseki" [The most female candidates since the war, 86% born in the
postwar era: Candidate analysis]. August 19. http://www.yomiuri.co.jp/election/
shugiin2009/news2/20090819-OYT1T00039.htm (accessed August 20, 2009).

Yoshida, S. (1961). *The Yoshida Memoirs: The Story of Japan in Crisis*. London:
Heinemann.

Yoshida, S., N. Hiroshi, and K. Yoshida (2007). *Yoshida Shigeru: Last Meiji Man*.
Lanham, MD: Rowman and Littlefield.

Zaller, J. (1992). *The Nature and Origins of Mass Opinion*. Cambridge:
Cambridge University Press.

INDEX

Note: Page numbers in *italics* indicate figures; those with a *t* indicate tables.